There Must Be A Reason

THERE MUST BE A REASON

Gilbert Anderson

Foreword by
Barbara Nichols, RMN

The Book Guild Ltd
Sussex, England

This book is sold subject to the condition that it shall not, by way of trade or otherwise, be lent, re-sold, hired out, photocopied or held in any retrieval system or otherwise circulated without the publisher's prior consent in any form of binding or cover other than that in which this is published and without a similar condition including this condition being imposed on the subsequent purchaser.

The Book Guild Ltd.
25 High Street,
Lewes, Sussex

First published 1993
© Gilbert Anderson 1993
Set in Baskerville
Typesetting by Southern Reproductions (Sussex)
East Grinstead, Sussex
Printed in Great Britain by
Antony Rowe Ltd.
Chippenham, Wiltshire.

A catalogue record for this book is
available from the British Library

ISBN 0 86332 834 2

CONTENTS

List of Centre Section Photographs		6
Foreword		7
Appreciation		8
Preface		9
Chapter 1	The wonder of healing	11
Chapter 2	My early days	15
Chapter 3	In the Second World War	32
Chapter 4	Miracles and mediumship	43
Chapter 5	Physical mediumship	54
Chapter 6	Branching out	72
Chapter 7	Involvement with the NFSH	81
Chapter 8	We move to Norfolk again – then back to London	93
Chapter 9	Research, removal and rivalry	117
Chapter 10	Psychic surgery	132
Chapter 11	What the healers say	148
Chapter 12	A new door opens	165
Chapter 13	Moving on from the NFSH	189
Chapter 14	Looking after ourselves at last	207

LIST OF CENTRE SECTION PHOTOGRAPHS

Ruth Anderson – serious illnesses overcome by healing after medical help failed.
Ruth and Gilbert welcoming guests at the Home Counties Association of Spiritual Healers Annual Dinner.
Laying on of hands following a demonstration in London by the late Harry Edwards.
Gilbert and Ruth Anderson, Harry Edwards, Olive and George Burton.
National Federation of Spiritual Healing Summer School at Overmead Hotel, Torquay, 1970.
Friday night is party night at the end of Summer School. Seen here Gilbert with his Troupe of Male Fairies.
The Denton Sanctuary.
Outlook from Sanctuary and waiting room.
New signs of life from our first pilot groups of cancer patients.
Cancer group in Nature Cure Clinic, London, showing the Biofeedback Instrument.
Gilbert healing a patient prior to her hundredth birthday.
World Federation of Healing stand, at Festival of Mind, Body and Spirit, London.

FOREWORD

Gilbert Anderson is the most humble man I have ever met, and on reading the proofs of this book, he has again been very modest. Many people in England and the continent could have given testimonials had they been asked as to the help given to them from Gilbert's great gift to relieve the suffering of mankind.

This book has only been written because of constant pressure from our friends in spirit, his wife Ruth, myself and many friends.

I always count it as a great privilege that I was allowed to work with 'Dear Gilly' in the healing room.

Barbara Nichols, RMN (Nicky)

APPRECIATION

I would like to express my appreciation to Ruth who has shared over sixty years of her life with me, Marjorie and Sid McQuillan for their tireless efforts with the manuscript, Charles and Viviane Simon-Laier, Elly and Jack Nickson, André Kind and Irene Beidemann who helped to make this publication possible, and to Barbara Nichols and the late Marcus McCausland who pressured me into writing it.

PREFACE

'Why should it happen to me?' A rather hackneyed saying by many people, particularly with regard to ill health, but it is necessary to use it in a slightly different vein to explain the title of this book and the many experiences the author and his wife have been subjected to. Extraordinary to many people, yet seemingly part of our everyday life as two very ordinary folk.

Talking of some of these experiences people have said, 'I would give my right arm to have had some of the opportunities you have had', yet to us, many we felt as a duty or a bit of a bind because we had long passed the time when we needed proof of the after-life and the wonderful power of psychic phenomena.

It was not until the Second World War that a series of inexplicable happenings began to enter our lives and completely change our whole future, but with all things there has to be a beginning, and so I leave you to share some of these experiences with us.

1

THE WONDER OF HEALING

When healing is discussed it is usually in the context of the overcoming of a physical condition. But what of the innumerable cases where medicine has failed to produce the desired result and other forms of healing have succeeded? There are so many possibilities to explore from which we can sometimes gain valuable knowledge by understanding some of these seemingly mysterious happenings.

Firstly, we must accept that each individual is unique, and will react to life, health and situations in their own way, and this will be governed largely by one's makeup. Faced with a particular problem we will each react to it in our own individual way – some successfully, some not so successfully – while others will see it as an insurmountable situation that they are quite unable to deal with. This will then set up a chain reaction of worry, anxiety, fear and a feeling of hopelessness at not being able to solve the problem. So we begin to see that we do not all come out of the same mould – even in families there are distinct variations – and we each express ourselves in our own way. This is fine for those who can cope with most of the problems in their lives, where they either face up to them and deal with them in a positive and constructive way, or let them 'roll off their shoulders' with reasonable unconcern.

But what of the many unfortunate people who just cannot cope? Unfortunately, we British are brought up to hide our feelings. We must 'put on a bold front' or 'keep a stiff upper lip' and in no way must we show our true feelings, with the result that these unfortunate people have to suppress their natural feelings, and try to present a very false image to the world at large. How often do we hear remarks like: 'He/she is a totally different person at home to what he/she is at work'? Emotions then, and how one is able to deal with them, are fundamentally important to health, and it is hoped that this book will help some of the 'worriers' to come to terms with their problems, and look at them as necessary experience from which they can learn to improve the quality of their lives, and so generate better health through a happier state of mind. The basis of all healing is love and compassion, and we should not be afraid to extend that love and compassion to ourselves. We are very remarkable people – when one considers all the many complexities of our makeup, the wonderful construction and function of our physical body, and its controlling influence, the brain and mind, plus the divine spark of God that gave us our being. So love this wonderful work of God, and give it the care and respect it is entitled to by learning to understand its many facets. What then is the recipe for good health and happiness?

1. Love, that is, unselfish love.
2. Peace of mind.
3. Sensible diet.
4. Reasonable exercise.
5. Live in the present, learn from the past, and look to a happy and fulfilling future.

Many people have been healed by osteopathy, acupuncture, chiropractics, herbalism, radionics, homoeopathy, and other complementary therapies when allopathic medicine has failed. Just as psychotherapy and hypnotherapy have been of great benefit to people with mental and emotional problems, and spiritual healing for the more subtle 'inner being' – the eternal part of us that does not die, and it is in these latter areas of our being that many of our problems originate. Sickness and suffering are often disguised forms of blessing because, in so many instances, one has time to assess one's priorities, recognise one's faults and failings, and appreciate the many blessings that have hitherto been taken for granted.

I am sad for the people who are convinced that this life is the 'be all and end all' of existence, and that there is no continuing life after death. What a dreadful waste of this marvellous mechanism we call 'us' – just to survive a given number of years striving for material riches and power. It would seem the more one seeks material wealth through greed rather than love, the more misery is created. The richer they become, the meaner they become, living in fear of losing this power they have attained – often at the expense of others. On the other hand, there is the humble little soul, with very few material possessions, perfectly content with his or her lot, having the time to evaluate life's true riches. He or she expresses love – not the selfish, possessing love that one so often meets with, but a desire and willingness to give loving help and understanding where it is most needed without wondering 'what can I get out of this?' I believe this person is the possessor of the greatest riches because he or she has found God within him or herself. And we all have the same God force within us. But for many people a very thick layer of materialism has been built over this God force so that we are not even aware of its existence.

How then do we peel back these layers of materialism? A greater understanding of our wholeness – the realisation that we are not just a physical manifestation, but that we express this wholeness on the more subtle levels of our being – the mental, emotional and spiritual expressions, are all part of this wonderfully complete us.

This awareness may sometimes come about through surgery when, during the period of anaesthesia, the spirit becomes 'loosened' from the physical body, and the patient becomes more aware of the spiritual part of his or her other makeup. During this period, while the brain is inactive, the mind is given the opportunity of bringing a fuller understanding of the purpose of life from this spiritual source.

Sometimes this awareness may come in the form of a spiritual revelation during a dream, or similar experience, when one feels or sees the Christ presence, bringing the conviction of a much fuller, richer, spiritual life, inspiring its practical application in this material world.

Very often, however, it is brought about through periods of illness and suffering, when one has plenty of time to look back over one's life, and evaluate what has been achieved during those years. What sort of person have I been? Could I perhaps have been a little more understanding of the other persons' point of view? Need I have been so critical of others? What good have I really done? So, with this time to analyse oneself, we often come to realise that we have been rather selfish and we could have been more loving. If we had not been so impatient, we could have understood the other person's point of view. With this period of learning about oneself, we have the incentive to try and improve the picture in the future. With illness, we can do this by being a better patient, not being so demanding, being appreciative of all that is done for me, and trying to be a bit brighter, and make the task of those looking after me a little easier by being as cheerful and cooperative as possible.

And what of suffering? Here again, one has the chance to evaluate one's life – the first questions always seem to be 'What have I done to deserve this?'; 'Why should it happen to me?'; or, 'Oh God, why make me suffer like this?'. It is so easy to blame someone else for our misfortunes, but are they always misfortunes? I think not. Is it right to blame God? After all, he has given us this body, this life, the ability to think and reason for ourselves and to make our own decisions, but put into this situation we accept none of these responsibilities. This seems to be one of our human frailties.

We were taught by one of our wise spiritual counsellors many years ago: 'It is through pain that we grow', and how very true that has proved to be to so many people, including myself. When one speaks to people who have gone through long periods of pain and suffering, it may seem hard to understand when they say: 'I thank God for my illness, because it has taught me so much about myself, and life as a whole. I have seen facets of myself that I never dreamed existed. It's a wonderful experience, and one that I would hate to have missed. I now have a real purpose to my life – it's marvellous.'

When one can speak from personal experience, it is done with conviction! I know – I have experienced pain and suffering myself. So, let me tell you how these experiences proved to be a blessing to both my wife and myself, and how our lives were changed from mere existence to the most rewarding fulfilment of God's love and compassion.

2

MY EARLY DAYS

When I left school my headmaster said to me: 'You will regret wasting this last year of schooling, my boy, you will look back on your school days as the happiest days of your life.' Some sixty odd years later, I still disagree with his prediction. Apart from the basic three Rs I have learned far more since leaving school than I did during those formative (or restrictive, as I thought of them) years.

I vividly remember my first day at school – I was literally dragged there kicking and screaming by my paternal grandmother. We were met by the headmistress, and I was handed over like the lamb to the slaughter. She took my hand muttering something like 'He'll be all right with me dear', and whisked me away with no more ado. She was tall and thin and, as I gazed up at her face, she looked about ten feet tall, and I wondered if it was colder up there than down where I was. I had heard my father saying once that the higher you got up in the sky the colder it got. On reflection, it could not have been so bad because I went next day without so much of a struggle.

My infant school days from then on are a little bit hazy. Then I moved up into the elementary school which was next door, and I cannot help comparing the present day youngster who is taken to school by car, sometimes very short distances, while I had four miles to walk in all weathers.

I was not particularly brilliant, preferring to use my hands rather than my brain. In comparison, my elder brother Ralph was the cat's whiskers. He won a scholarship to the London Polytechnic, wore an Eton suit and mortarboard, and really was the pride of the family.

At the age of nine my parents decided that to keep me out of mischief I should either learn to play the piano or join the church choir. The piano teacher lived next door and because I did not like her son I opted for the choir. We were a fine bunch of angelic monsters but I liked singing and worked my way up through the ranks to become joint top boy and soloist. These were happy days filled with the odd boyish pranks such as loosely tying two door knockers together, knocking on one door and hiding, and when the first door was opened it pulled the knocker on the second door, the first one finding no one there shut the door as the second door was opened. We choir boys had our practice in the evening early and the men followed on when we had finished. Often we would amuse ourselves by mixing up the men's hats and coats and hiding the odd one or two to add to the general confusion, or creep in one of the side doors of the church and bombard the men during their practice with wads of paper shot at them with rubber bands.

At the age of eleven I had to sit examinations for either the grammar school or county secondary school, not expecting to pass either. However, although I did not get what I wanted, which was the grammar school, I did get into the rather posh county secondary school.

These were the years of the First World War. My father was in the army and we had, of necessity, to make do and mend in lots of ways particularly with entertainment and toys. One of the most popular toys at that time – for kids with wealthier parents than we lesser mortals – was called 'The Flying Dutchman'. It was a vehicle on four wheels, about three feet long with a seat over the rear axle, the front axle pivoted and was steered by the feet. Two vertical hand levers were linked to a cranked back axle. The two hand levers moved back and forth driving the flyer at quite considerable speeds and this was where I used a little ingenuity. I told my brother we could make one up for ourselves and he was very enthusiastic. We found an old baby's pushchair, dismantled it, using the wheels and one axle for the front, fixing this to a pivot in the centre which was, in turn, attached to a plank of wood three feet long by fifteen inches wide at the rear, reducing to six inches forward to allow for a foot either side for steering. A local blacksmith made us up the cranked back axle and linkage for nothing praising our ingenuity, and the hand levers we made out of bits from the pushchair, and thus we were in business. In 1917 these Flyers cost £20, which was a fortune then. Ours cost one week's pocket money for each of us, a total of one shilling and we got endless enjoyment out of it. There was one restriction to it, however, for us, because only one could use it at a time and we wanted something we could enjoy together. Then we had another bright idea.

Our sister had an old bicycle which had been lying in the garden rusting for a long time, so we decided to have a look at it and see what could be done with it. The tyres were rotten so we took them off; the frame, saddle, chain and pedals were all right, so we gave the bicycle a good oiling and it seemed all right. Our house backed on to the railway and, coming out of the house, turning right 100 yards up the road another road went off at right angles over the railway bridge, and continued on in a gradual incline for half a mile. The idea was for us both to ride on the bicycle down the hill, and see how far we could get without pedalling, one sitting on the saddle and the other standing on the pedals steering. So at five o'clock one morning we got it out, pushed it the half mile up the hill all set for our adventure. We had already decided on who should sit and who should stand and take command – I was in the saddle and Ralph took charge. Off we went making an awful noise with the wheels stripped of their tyres but, nothing daunted, this was our day and half way down the hill we were really going at a fair speed. I said to Ralph, 'Put the brakes on a bit boy or we'll go straight through the houses at the bottom', but the reply, as it whizzed past on the wind was, 'I've got them on but they don't work.' The junction over the railway bridge was looming ever nearer and we had a ninety degree left turn to make at any moment. I am not sure what Ralph's thoughts were at this stage, but I was trying to decide which would be best – to be spread on the wall of one of the houses, or go through the window into the sitting room. Over the bridge and we were there – leaning hard over to the left we raced round in an arc and slid along the curb (which had only been laid two weeks before) with sparks flying from the metal rims and stone curb. But strangest of all was that we were still on the bicycle and cruising on past our house for a good quarter of a mile before an incline enabled us to dismount by ourselves.

We pushed it back home deciding that it probably was doing less harm rusting in the garden.

Beyond the railway on to which our house backed was a wood stretching for about one and a half miles and this was our favourite playground. Tree climbing was the most popular activity and we became quite expert at swinging from branch to branch and on from tree to tree, ending with a competition to see who could travel furthest without touching the ground. This was good fun but rather hard on our clothes. I remember one occasion when my paternal grandparents were staying with us. They seemed very staid people, perfectly dressed and always referred to by my parents as 'mater and pater'. I came home with a tear in my pants, received a hiding from my mother, and was most surprised to hear my grandmother say 'Oh come now Jessie, he's only being a boy. I'll mend them.'

My most vivid memory of the war was seeing from the bedroom window one evening a Zeppelin being attacked by one of our fighter planes. Shortly afterwards it burst into flames and we watched fascinated as the flames spread from its centre, finally breaking in half and falling to the ground only a few miles from our home. Early next morning we cycled out to see the wreckage and were astonished to find the great number of people who had got there before us. We had to be satisfied with a burned piece of tunic with a button on it and a few twisted pieces of metal as souvenirs, somewhat disappointing but there was still great excitement when we showed them at school.

Another hair-raising adventure we engaged in involved a footbridge over the railway near our home. This had steel strutted girders in its construction. The top girders on either side were four inches wide and we would dare each other to walk across on one of those girders with a twenty foot drop down on to the line below. After a while this got too easy, so we decided to do it when a train went through, just as the engine belched its smoke up at us. Another variation on this simple pastime was to try and drop a stone down the funnel as it went through and, if we managed to time it right, it would shoot out like a shot from a gun.

On a much more sedate note, one of our Saturday pastimes was to cycle to the Manor House from our home in Palmers

Green to see the horses pulling the trams up the hill. This was before there were such things as electric trams. Arriving at the top, the spare horse would be unhitched to wait for the next tram to go down the hill. There was a flat platform on the front and back of the tram on to which the horse would be led and have a free ride down the hill ready to pull the next one up.

I have already mentioned my paternal grandparents, who were Londoners, but my maternal grandparents were quite different. They were Granny and Grandad. Grandad was a miller in Bedfordshire, a big bearded cuddly bear of a man and, as a child, I would sit on his knee playing with his beard and he used to say, 'You'll never be a man until you've grown a beard me boy.' I would stay at the Mill with them in my holidays, and loved the country and the pleasant easy way of life. One thing that I found hard to understand was that on Sunday morning Grandad would get out the pony and trap and drive off, but I was never allowed to go with him. Then at about three o'clock in the afternoon he would return, but he was always asleep in the trap when he came home. This puzzled me for a long time until I learned later that he made a circuit of all the pubs for several miles around, and at the last one they put him in the trap and the pony brought him home unaided.

Another holiday I remember there was when I contracted chicken pox which spoiled it for me – most unfair for that to happen to me on my holiday. Granny was a typical country lovable Granny, spoiled us rotten and we loved it.

Going to the toilet there was quite an event – nothing indoors, but involved a trip of about thirty yards, often in the dark with an oil lamp, down the garden to 'the shed' which was a three-seater (two large and one small). You could almost imagine the family sitting down together.

My main interests at school were art, woodwork and science, none of which I seemed to get much help with, but was rather left to my own devices. If you were doing reasonably well, the art master would almost ignore you, but if anything was wrong he would tell you so but not say how to correct it. The woodwork master was a Welshman with a temper, and we learned to be quick because, if he wanted to attract our attention, he would pick up the nearest tool and throw it at us.

However, the science master really taught us something, which was how to make stink bombs and gunpowder amongst other things, and this is where I really came into my own. My choirboy friend Ginger was at another school, and had not reached these dizzy heights of scientific discovery, so I grew another foot in his estimation. We decided to make a noise, or name, for ourselves, so we started, quite correctly, in a small way. Using a hollow shaft key and a nail, each tied on the end of a piece of string twelve inches long, gunpowder was stuffed into the hollow shaft of the key, the nail pushed in after it, then knocked against a wall causing an explosion. This was all right, but we wanted to progress so we moved on step by step with progressively larger keys and nails until we finally arrived at the vestry door key of the church, and a six inch nail. This explosion blew a brick out of the house wall.

Ginger and I were still ambitious and needed to improve in the explosives field, so why not fill a tobacco tin with explosive, seal it, and put it on the tramline? THE TRAMS WERE NOW ELECTRIC!! We deftly placed the tin on the tramline, hid behind a hedge to wait for the tram to come along (the trams at that time had a set of four bogey wheels front and rear of the body). When the tram came along there was a loud bang and also the explosion blew the front bogeys off the rails, and the whole tram was slewed ninety degrees across both tracks. Fortunately, no one was hurt, but we were so frightened we took to our heels and did not stop until we had gone through the one and a half miles of wood behind the house. Needless to say there was plenty of speculation for several weeks, but the culprits were never identified although, no doubt, some had their suspicions as to who it might have been.

The time was fast approaching when I would leave school, and go out into the big world of business. My only ambition had been to become a cartoon artist on a national newspaper, but this idea my father ruled out straight away. It was far too precarious an occupation to be even considered, but a safe job in an office was thought to be suitable. My elder brother was working in the offices of a paper manufacturers, Wiggins Teape and Company, in Aldgate, and it was decided that I should go there as well. I did and hated every moment of it.

Licking stamps, making tea, and running errands, did not seem to me to be the height of my ambition, and it was a most uninteresting way of spending my days. I became very aware that my name was Anderson. Every few minutes I heard called out, 'Anderson come here, take this to Mr So-and-So.'

I struck up a friendship with one chap in the office, Laurie Metcalf – he was six feet two inches tall and I was five feet two inches tall and it was not long before we were known as 'Mut and Geoff' after two comedians of that day – one tall and thin, the other short and fat – although I was not fat. In 1921 I had spent a holiday on the Norfolk Broads yachting with a party and enjoyed it very much, and talked Laurie into trying it too. I had a motorbike and liked trials and scrambles, with plenty of mud and water. Laurie had a Morgan three-wheeler, so we had a few weekends on the Norfolk Broads during the summer, leaving the office at five o'clock on a Friday, driving straight up to Wroxham where we picked up a yacht; then leaving at six o'clock on a Monday morning, to be back in the office for nine o'clock. When we were not on the Broads we went to Hoddesdon in Hertfordshire. 'Dobbs Weir' was a favourite bathing spot on the river, and we had a little hut on an island until it became so crowded we decided to look for somewhere else. We found a very nice spot about three miles upstream at Fishers Green, and persuaded the farmer to rent us a piece of land on the riverside. We built a wooden chalet on this, and had some very pleasant weekends there, bathing and just lazing about.

One lunchtime we were ambling up Aldgate High Street with a little time on our hands when suddenly Laurie stopped and pointed up to the roof of a building opposite – 'What is it?' I said, 'Nothing' was the reply, 'I just want to see how nosey people are.' And sure enough, in no time at all a large crowd had gathered gazing up at nothing. Having achieved his object we just melted away and left them to it. On another occasion, we had just come out of a jewellers in Aldgate High Street, as two girls walked past and, just as they passed us, something slid down the legs of one of them and we realised her knickers had fallen down. Without any hesitation she deftly stepped out of them and walked on. Laurie, always the perfect gentleman, picked them up, hurried after her, handing them over saying, 'Excuse me miss, you dropped your handkerchief.' That incident developed into a friendship which finally resulted in their marriage.

During these office days we decided to join the Territorial Army, and picked the Westminster Dragoons because it sounded quite 'posh'. This had been a Cavalry Brigade which, shortly after we joined, was transferred to the 22nd London Armoured Car Co. attached to the Royal Tank Regiment. We had solid tyred armoured cars, each weighing twenty tons, which we drove from London to Lulworth in Dorset for our summer camps.

Transport generally was not very comfortable anywhere in those days. To get to work from Palmers Green meant a tram to Wood Green, then a Tilling Stevens Petrol Electric Bus to Liverpool Street, and then walk through to Aldgate. These buses too had solid tyres, open top with wooden seats and tarpaulin sheets for if it rained. A little later two brothers made a great impact by introducing a bus with pneumatic tyres. This was heralded as a 'pirate' bus service which ran from Enfield to Aldgate. This bus was very successful because it was more comfortable. However, after they had been running this service for six months the London General Omnibus Company had it withdrawn. Unfortunately this meant back to the wretched Tilling Stevens boneshakers again.

Just to add to the local chaos, the first National Transport Strike was called. This meant I had to walk ten miles each way to and from work. So, for a whole week I walked twenty miles a day to get to a job I didn't like! However, a week or two later when walking in Aldgate East I saw a bicycle shop displaying a racing bike in the window at a price that seemed quite reasonable. I did my sums quickly and decided I could just about afford it without having to pay bus fares, so I went in next day and bought it. This saved a lot of transport problems, and I got to work quicker than by bus.

Also around this time, I began to be impressed by, and wanted to impress, girls. One of my friends had a younger sister who I saw from time to time, but had not paid much attention to. However, when I saw her some time later I saw that she had become a very attractive girl, and I started taking her out. Our relationship fluctuated a bit with other girls and boys in the pipeline. She was an excellent dancer while I, in comparison, had two left feet, so she was naturally attracted to boys who could dance well. After we had both had time to sort ourselves out we got together in a more serious relationship without any further interest in anyone else on either side. We each got on very well with the others' parents, and I was always made very welcome in her home where I began to spend more and more of my spare time. On her eighteenth birthday we decided to get engaged. Ruth was the only girl in the family with four older brothers. She was not a healthy girl, often having abcesses in her ears, and I would sit with her quite late sometimes trying to soothe and comfort her. I can remember my mother saying when we became engaged that I was very silly to get myself involved with her, since she was a sick girl and I was courting trouble. (This year, God willing, we will have celebrated our Diamond Wedding, so it can't have been all bad.)

But here was I, in 1930 working in London for the princely sum of £5 per week, and a vague thought of marriage in the distance. Then my world began to change. My brother had left the office about a year before and had started a small business transporting eggs from East Anglian Farmers to Express and United Dairies in London. This had grown over the year and another vehicle would soon be required. He asked me if I would like to join him. Just to get away from the office and out into the country would be marvellous, and more money into the bargain, so I agreed. An additional van was duly bought and I left the Aldgate office without a single regret – and now for the open road.

I reminded my brother that I had never driven four-wheelers before, only motorbikes, to which he replied: 'Oh it's dead easy and you can't fall off it either.' So I had half an hour's practice up and down the road, then set off on a 250 mile trip into East Anglia. Finding farms for the first time in unknown territory is not the easiest thing in the world but I managed, and the round trip took me fifteen hours, but I had done it without any problems. Once having found my way around it was much easier, and the overall journey time was cut to about twelve hours.

As time went on the business continued to expand, with new calls to be made almost every week, our time away from home got longer and longer, with time in bed less and less, until it became an event if we got to bed more than once a week. This was beginning to present problems, my courting became almost non-existent, and it was getting harder and harder keeping awake driving at night. On one occasion I remembered driving into Thetford in Norfolk. My next awareness was driving out of what I thought was Thetford only to realise it was Ware on the outskirts of London – I had no recollection of those fifty miles in between. On another occasion I felt very drowsy, pulled off the road to close my eyes for a few minutes, and was fast asleep. I woke up suddenly to see a telegraph pole right in front of me, heard and felt the engine running, stamped on the brakes only to find I was stationary anyway.

Fog can be a problem, particularly in the Fens. However, with a commercial vehicle visibility is much better because the driver sits well above the lights, and you do not get the glare throwback. Our depot was on the North Circular Road at Palmers Green, and one morning getting home about eight-thirty I pulled into our yard and the fog was still thick, got out of the lorry and found cars immediately behind me. There was a string of about a dozen and some had followed me from Ely and Cambridge.

Our weekly programme was on Monday to collect from the farms; on Tuesday to deliver in London to an ever-increasing number of customers, some living well out in the suburbs, often friends of a farmer, and often a very small consignment into the bargain. Returning to the depot we would load up the vehicles with returnable boxes and crates to exchange for full ones the next day, fill up with petrol, oil and water, check tyres, and see that everything was ready for a four o'clock start the next morning. Wednesday to Thursday was a repeat of this procedure, and Friday too. The only difference on Saturday was that we washed and greased the vehicles giving them a complete checkover to ensure everything was in order, including changing, or replacing, tyres if necessary. One Saturday evening my brother came back to the depot long after everything should have been done and the vehicles garaged, to find mine still out in the yard. There was no sign of me outside or inside the garage, but he finally found me fast asleep under the vehicle, where I had fallen asleep in the middle of greasing.

After the servicing on Saturdays we could either load up ready for early Monday morning, or leave that part until Sunday morning. By this time I had a ten ton Dennis which was the largest of the fleet, and took that much longer to service and load, so I usually opted for loading on Sunday morning. Having done this, I would go home to bath and change, then off to Ruth's for Sunday lunch. This was about our only time of meeting now. Our proposed matrimony was looking a bit precarious, especially after I had fallen asleep over Sunday lunch with her family, and repeated the performance when I spent Christmas Day with her family.

We decided that, with this rather hit and miss relationship we would be better off married, and started seriously thinking about possible dates, and where we would live. Having decided on a date six months hence, one of her brothers who had been engaged for eighteen months, thought he must get in first, and fixed his own wedding for three months before ours. Time quickly went by. Ruth was an only daughter, and the apple of her father's eye, so she was to have the best – top hat and tails, nothing less would be considered. Two days before the wedding my pride and joy, a Morgan three-wheeler, decided to break down, and I had planned to go down to Devon in it for our honeymoon. This threw all of our plans completely, so last minute changes were made, and we decided to go by train to Herne Bay. That settled, we had to make arrangements for our 'get away'. We had given her brother and his bride a hard time, and I knew what would be cooking up for us. Fortunately no one knew where we were going. We had arranged for a car to take us away after the reception, also for another belonging to friends, to be about a quarter of a mile away, where we could make a swap knowing that the car to take us from the house would be decorated with everything that was available. We had got a flat, the top half of a semi-detached house in Palmers Green, and we led people to believe we would spend the first night there.

The great day came – 4 June 1932 – and all went well with the ceremony, reception over and we were ready for the off. We fought our way to the car which, as we had expected, had everything on it bar the kitchen sink – covered in confetti and rice, we finally got in the car and were away. Looking back, as we drove off, the last thing we saw was Ruth's old Nannie,

'Aunt Rose', picking up her new hat which she had bought specially for the wedding, trying to straighten it out. It had been knocked off in the general turmoil and the car had run over it. Our change over satisfactorily completed, we brushed ourselves down, and settled in for a comfortable ride to Charing Cross. We already had our tickets and, on arrival, we went into the refreshment bar for a few minutes before catching the train.

We were just leaving to go across to the platform when I saw spatted feet below a notice board running towards our train. We pulled back out of sight, and watched with baited breath, as our pursuers went the whole length of the train. Not finding us there they concluded that our friends must have given them false information and, fortunately for us, they left the station just giving us time to catch the train. They did, however, have one success. I do not know who, or how, but someone got to our suitcase and, when we opened it in the bedroom, confetti shot out everywhere. Until then we had felt quite confident that we would not be recognised as newlyweds on our honeymoon.

After the wedding Ruth's father shut himself away because he was so upset that his girl had gone. And he was so upset that her parents rang us the following day to say they were coming down to see us. They came and, having satisfied themselves that she was all right and, with the reassurance that she would still pop in to see them at home, life settled down peacefully again and, in keeping with this, the weather which had been so cold on our wedding day, also improved, getting warmer.

A number of people who knew us individually were sure our marriage would not last. In fact my friend, Ruth's brother, gave us six months at most. Strange, but we have survived our Silver, Ruby and Golden anniversaries, with the Diamond within striking distance, so it could not have been that bad.

Our first home was, as I have mentioned, an upstairs flat – not wholly self-contained – we had the upstairs, and the owners the downstairs, sharing the bathroom. We had gone to Wards Stores in Tottenham for our furniture, and furnished the lounge-diner, bedroom and kitchen for £100.

Ruth and I occupied the flat for a year until the government introduced new laws limiting driving hours on commercial vehicles. This meant major changes in our firm's operating, requiring us to have a depot in Norfolk as well as London. It was decided that I would move up to Norfolk and Ralph would stay in London. We found a suitable depot in Wymondham which was central for our collecting and also for the nightly trunk service we would have to introduce. Our official opening at Wymondham was 1 January, but the house we were moving into was not quite completed, so I went up on my own, and Ruth joined me a short while later. Having settled into our new home, with much shorter working hours, I found it quite difficult adjusting to a more normal sleep routine and, for a while, after lying awake for several hours, I would suggest we got the car out and have a spin to Yarmouth. We would do this and have a walk along the seafront, drive home, have a fry up, then sleep for an hour or two. Our only near neighbours must have thought us mad at first. They lived next door and were Jack, who was an insurance agent, his wife Topsy, and their massive Alsatian dog called Rex, as big as a donkey and very, very aggressive. As Topsy was left alone a lot Rex, the dog, had been trained to be protective, and he certainly was. If we spoke to him over the fence his lip would curl back, and an awful snarl would be his response. After a while we could talk to him without being snarled at but, put your hand over the top of the fence, and you stood a good chance of losing it. I remember one day there had been some trouble in the town and with our business I tried to be on friendly terms with the police, and we had come back with news of a burglary in the town, saw Topsy in her front room, and went in the garden to tell her about it. She opened the window and, as we were talking Rex jumped up and, without thinking, I put out my hand to stroke him then, after a few seconds, realised it was still attached to my arm and still in one piece. Topsy was delighted at this and felt sure we could now come into the house, and he would accept us as friends. We weren't so sure. However, a week or so later we did go in. Rex was shut in the kitchen until we had settled in the lounge. He was then brought in and, when his lip was settled back into a more composed state, we were told to sit perfectly still while he sniffed around to get to know us. Have you ever had a head, bigger than your own, with a cold wet nose, fanned with hot breath, pushed into your face, moving steadily all over your person from head to toe – missing nothing? Finally, after what seemed like a lifetime, he was satisfied that we were safe to leave alone, and we were accepted as welcome guests.

We found making friends with the local folk very difficult with just a few exceptions. Having become friendly with some of the police, I was invited to become a member of the Observer Corps, a branch of the Special Constabulary, detecting enemy aircraft in the event of hostilities. This was quite new and the equipment very amateurish. The equipment consisted of a circular table approximately two feet in diameter marked off with the compass points. In the centre of the table was a vertical post with string attached to its top, and the whole table was mounted on a tripod. The string would be lined up in the direction of the aircraft, and the angle with it lined up to where the aircraft was, to estimate its height and speed. We would meet once a month for practice when the RAF or local flying club would send up the odd plane for us to practice on. There were only six of us on the post, and we had a field telephone to report back to the Centre in Norwich. One of the members was a shopkeeper in the town, and he was also fire chief. This sounded grand, but the fire tender was a small trailer carrying a water tank and pump, and this he towed behind his car. As I said, all very amateurish.

Ruth was a very attractive girl and well dressed, and before long gossip was flying and we found that life in a small market town community was not always easy.

We had an agreement, Ralph and I, concerning breakdowns at night. The halfway between our London and Norfolk depots was Six Mile Bottom near Newmarket. North of this mark I would be called out and south of it Ralph. At two am one morning the phone rang, it was the truck driver, he'd broken down just my side of the Six Mile Bottom railway crossing.

'Have you checked all the obvious possible faults?' I asked.

'Oh, yes, everything seems to be OK. I've been over everything.'

So, off I set on a fifty mile trek to see what I could do to get him on his way. On arrival I checked the electricals, and there was no energy getting through. The starter motor was dead, no lights or any sign of life. Going to the first source of all electrical life, the battery – one of the leads was hanging loose. I put it back on and everything was perfectly OK, a simple obvious fault, so easily detectable, cost me a night's sleep and one hundred miles unnecessary drive.

We were being affected by growing competition in our business and money was getting tighter so, to economise, Ruth and I moved into a smaller house, sold my Morris 8, which had been my pride and joy, and bought an old Austin 7, which we called Bouncing Billy. It went along rather like a rubber ball. This I could cope with but it had a 'thing' about approaching traffic – as soon as it got near to anything coming towards us it had a terrific urge to embrace it. I really had to work hard to get it going where I wanted – which was straight ahead. We made one trip to London in it in ice and fog, and that was it, it had to go. We then bought a Clyno from a farmer friend. It was a big, old thing, but very comfortable, and did us well for a time. During this year business became so cut-throat, we decided to get out. We left Norfolk and took a house in Upminster, Essex, where I had been offered a job as sales representative for an oil company, and Ralph started up a second-hand car sales business in North London.

My territory was the whole of Essex. There was a senior sales manager over all of East Anglia whom I only saw once when I started. East Anglia is referred to as the travellers' graveyard because of the distances between towns, and time lost getting from one to another. It was hard work, and a bit depressing sometimes, but I made the acquaintance of another sales representative selling car batteries. We struck up a very good and lasting friendship, and having the same customers, would often share cars – his one day and mine the next – thus having the benefit of each other's company, and cutting down on travel expenses.

In August, 1939, having built up a sizeable business connection I was summoned to head office and told that my turnover was not enough, and my services were no longer required. I found out later this was part of their policy, employ a junior representative to build up dead ground then when it was well established, pass it over to a senior representative who covered a much wider area, in this case the whole of East Anglia.

During my time with the company I had done business with

a small flying club on the Southend road, near Romford, and made some good friends there, spending most weekends with them giving flights at five shillings a time. There were four pilots and two Avro biplanes. At the end of the day we would go up to a small pub about a quarter of a mile away for a drink and bite to eat, before going home. The aircraft belonged to two of the boys. Jim Ford who had a garage and built his own plane, and Ronnie Jude whose plane had a large Donald Duck painted on the fuselage. He would amuse the onlookers by talking like Donald Duck when in the air. Often I would fly with him towards the end of the day when things got quiet. On one particular occasion we were having a last fling before closing for the day, doing a bit of stunt flying. Those on the ground were waving and shouting at us which we took to be encouragement, so we did a bit more then, as we landed, the port wing collapsed. The main spar had broken and this is what they were trying to tell us, they could see it moving.

On another occasion, it had been a very busy Sunday. They had all had enough, and Ronnie agreed to give the last flight, about fifteen minutes. I waited behind to help shut up shop when he'd finished, and the others went on up to the pub. Having finished his trip, he said, 'Come on, let's shoot up the pub!' So, off we went swooping down over the pub twice, but the second time we got a mite too close, and took off the chimney! We returned half an hour later on foot to find them clearing up soot and debris, and not in the best of tempers.

On leaving Norfolk I transferred to another Observer Corps Post in Essex. This was situated on the flat roof of the Telephone Exchange in Rainham, close to Hornchurch Aerodrome. Here the equipment was much more sophisticated, and we had good liaison with the RAF at Hornchurch, and some very useful exercises. There were more of us on this Post than in Wymondham, twelve in all, including my battery sales friend, Bill.

Our house in Upminster had a longish back garden, with a stream at the bottom. It was lawn for the most part and flower beds at the bottom. One evening Ruth and I were sitting out on the lawn facing down the garden relaxing and enjoying the sunset, when she nudged me saying, 'Can you see anything in the flowers?' I said, 'Yes, I can see lights moving about,' but thought I was imagining things. We had sometimes jokingly said, 'There are fairies at the bottom of my garden,' but this really was happening. As we watched, these lights began to take form – they were the little people one reads of in fairy tales. We walked stealthily nearer and, sure enough, these little figures were busily moving from plant to plant and bloom to bloom, as though they actually were lovingly tending them. We watched this, fascinated, until the chill of the evening drove us indoors. We saw them on several occasions but would not talk about it to anyone fearing they would think of us as 'a bit odd' to say the least.

3

IN THE SECOND WORLD WAR

In September 1939 we had been visiting friends in Kent, and had decided to go to the cinema in Dover when, in the middle of the programme, the news was flashed on the screen 'Britain has declared war on Germany - will all Territorial and Auxiliary service personnel report immediately to their respective Centres.' The cinema emptied like magic, and I went to the police station to see what I should do. We went home the next morning and I reported for duty at midday. There was a full complement of personnel and it was decided that we would work in pairs - one to work the plane-spotting instrument, and the other to report to our Centre. Our post, P2, was considered to be in an important position, both for the aerodrome and any enemy aircraft coming up the Thames to London. Some of our members found it difficult to fit in as much time as was needed to keep the post manned twenty-four hours a day so, one or two of us who were able to do more did twelve hours, four on four off, throughout the twenty-four.

Almost immediately after war was declared the Observer Corps was transferred from the police to the Royal Air Force and, although a voluntary service, we came under stricter control. We had aircraft recognition tests at regular intervals, and no doubt because we had more time together to practice, Bill and I always came out best, both for recognition and concise reporting to Centre. In between our duties on the Post, Bill and I were also Instructors in the Hornchurch ATC - myself on navigation and Bill on physical training.

During these early war years we had to install Anderson shelters. These were constructed of corrugated iron sunk into the ground with just the domed top above ground level, this being covered with the excavated earth. One of Ruth's brothers lived next door and he decided to have his shelter at the bottom of the garden as he did not want to spoil his lawn. We had decided to have ours near the house. His was finished first complete with a boarded floor and the next morning we were invited to inspect his handiwork. He opened the door, stepped in and sank in about two feet of water on which the wooden floor was floating. He had dug down below the level of the stream, and the water had found its own level. In spite of installing a pump it was always wet, so he had to move it further up the garden after all.

In 1940 finances became difficult and we had to move into a flat over the fifty-shilling tailors in Corbits Tey Road, opposite the recreation ground. We had a beautiful golden retriever called Carlo who Ruth often exercised in the recreation ground and, when the Army moved into Upminster, they drilled there. The Sergeant-Major took a fancy to Carlo, and asked if he could take him with them on their marches and on parade. So often he would go off with them, and earned some extra rations from their kitchen. Then one day, Ruth discovered that when taking the dog in one direction passing 'The Bell' public house he did not want to go past – he wanted to go in. We then found out that he had been taken in there after a march, and taught to salute for the King, an arrowroot biscuit and half a pint of beer. He was a very intelligent animal and, no matter how heavy the shopping basket was, he would insist on carrying it.

When the air raid warning sounded for the first time after we moved into the flat we felt pretty safe because it was constructed of reinforced concrete, with a staircase leading to the flat above. Under this concrete stair were two cupboards, one large and the other smaller, and we decided that these would be our air raid shelters, although we had an Anderson shelter in the garden. We showed Carlo the smaller cupboard saying, 'Now, when you hear the siren you go in there, and stay there until the all clear sounds.' We pushed him into it and then when the all clear sounded said, 'You can come out now when you hear that sound.' Some days later when the warning sounded, we were all set to get back in our shelter, but couldn't find Carlo until we looked in his cupboard. There he was, quite settled, and seemingly happy in his new bed. He never had to be told anything more than once. Ruth had taken a course on animal welfare, and was the ARP Warden for animals, going out with the vet, or police, looking for any stray or injured animals following or during an air raid, as need be.

Our Observer Post had been greatly improved. We had access to it by a ladder from inside the telephone exchange, through a trapdoor into a tank room, then out on to the roof which had a low brick wall on all sides. With raids hotting up we had been given a wooden hut rest room on the roof, with its walls lined with aircraft silhouettes. The instrument was positioned in the centre of the roof with a five foot sandbag surround. Being on duty together Bill and I had found ways of whiling away the time at night when no raids came our way. We brought along a primus stove, and would have a fry-up halfway through the night, as we sometimes did a double turn from midnight to eight o'clock. These hours would also be used for checking each other on aircraft, visual recognition and engine sound, together with position and estimated distance, direction and height without visual contact.

August 1940 really saw the German raids building up to the tremendous Battle of Britain when masses of German bombers came over looking like huge flocks of birds and, hovering around them, their fighter escort. As they neared the English coast we would hear other Observer Posts reporting their position until we could pick them up, when we took over. Our fighter strength was pitifully small compared with the masses of enemy aircraft they had to contend with, and we had the greatest admiration for those Hurricane pilots. Just a handful of lads, up into battle, down to rearm and refuel, then off again, sometimes going on almost continuously throughout the day. Often we would invite them to our flat in the evening and, on one occasion, after a particularly busy day, they came along and one started to fall asleep. The others said, 'For God's sake don't let Jimmy go to sleep. We'll never get him back.' But he fell asleep anyway and they had to carry him to the car. They were due to come again the next day but at nine o'clock in the evening one rang to say they wouldn't be coming, because three of the boys had 'bought it' that day and Jimmy was among them. It really was a 'here today gone tomorrow' situation until more aircraft and pilots were available.

Then the Germans started on London and the docks, hoards of them during the day and more than enough at night as well. It was strange, but if ever there was any activity near our Post, it was always Bill and me on duty. One particular afternoon heavy dog fighting had been going on when an ME 110 broke away and came hurtling towards us.

The pilot first let go a bomb, then machine-gun fire spattering all over the roof. Bill was reporting the incident to Centre in a rather excited voice, and the person at Centre said, 'All right, all right, calm down and talk a bit slower.' 'Calm down be b——' was Bill's reply, 'we're being dive bombed and machine-gunned.' While this was going on I had seen the bomb hit the road, just missing us. It bounced and was lost in the front garden of a house, without exploding. When things were quieter we had an inspection of the roof which was pock marked from the machine-gun attack, everywhere except where we had been standing. Why we should be spared when so many others were being killed was hard to understand.

On another occasion, I was going on duty at about eleven o'clock at night, and cycling because petrol was hard to come by. A German bomber had been stooging about over the aerodrome for several minutes until I was half way round the perimeter when I heard the bombs whistling down. They sounded uncomfortably near, so I threw the bicycle into the ditch and followed it. Seconds seem like hours when you are waiting for something nasty to happen. The first bomb hit and exploded, then the second. They were coming directly towards me. The third exploded and, making a quick assessment of distance between the craters clearly indicated that the fourth was due to fall directly on my patch. The only prayer I could think of then was, 'Oh, God, this is it. Dear God don't drag it out. Let's get it over with.' The fourth bomb never fell. There were two more explosions equidistant to each other, but they missed me. I have often asked myself, 'Why?' I suppose there must be a reason for these things but all I felt at the time was a tremendous relief that, for some unaccountable reason, I was still here. When the jelly had gone out of my legs I remounted my bicycle to resume the remaining three-quarters of a mile to the Post. Just turning a corner with a high hedge on my left, there was an almighty explosion and flash. I fell off my bike this time with fright, my thoughts being, 'Don't count your chickens.' Then I heard voices from the other side of the hedge, and they definitely were not Angel voices. It was an Ack Ack gun that had not been there before. Finally, arriving on the Post my friend was highly amused at my experience until, going home next morning, we paced out the distances between the craters and, had the fourth bomb fallen, it would have been right in my lap.

On the night raids the Germans would send out some bombers with incendiaries to light up the target, so that the main stream could then try and get their bombs on the same spots. There was extensive marsh land between us and the Thames and, during the Docks raids, decoy fires were lit to distract attention from the Docks area. We had a very poor respect for some German bomb aimers because they seldom got within half a mile of these targets. We were three-quarters of a mile away and stood more chance of being hit than the intended target.

Early one morning, just before light, there had been a little enemy movement, some searchlights and sporadic Ack Ack fire, but it had been comparatively quiet. We were talking and looking up and I saw an object floating towards us which we realised was a parachute mine. It hit the parapet, taking some of it with it as it scraped across the roof, and off the other side. It exploded half a mile further on demolishing an empty cottage. Again, I asked why it did not explode on that first impact with our roof instead of waiting until it was half a mile away. It must have hit several objects en route.

During those busy days at Hornchurch one of the pilots was seen to have been shot down and safely landed in France and, as soon as the CO, Group-Captain Broadhurst, heard this, he set off in a Miles Magister two-seater plane to see if he could pick him up. The Magister was very slow, and would be a very difficult target for the German fighter because of its slow speed and manoeuvrability. He wave hopped over and recovered a precious pilot.

The Observer Corps, although still voluntary, was upgraded and given the title Royal Observer Corps. Our instrument table was set out in a grid covering a ten mile diameter, and we could pinpoint most places of interest, such as our house, from it.

On one of the daylight raids on the aerodrome we saw considerable damage done both to the aerodrome buildings and aircraft on the ground. One Spitfire received a direct hit just as it was taking off to intercept. As I said, we did not hold some German bomb aimers in a very high esteem and, on this occasion, bombs were dropping in Upminster two miles off target. One of these explosions had me worried because it was too close to our flat for comfort. I tried to contact the police but the telephone line was damaged, and I had to wait another one and a half hours before getting home to see whether Ruth was safe. I arrived amidst some confusion because the bomb had exploded in the school playground just behind the flat. Ruth had been persuaded to use the Anderson shelter by the police, rather than the cupboard under the stairs, and earth from the school playground had landed on the shelter sealing her in. Ruth had just been rescued when I arrived. That was the one and only time the shelter was used.

By mid 1942 the Allies had proved their supremacy in the air, and German bombing had almost come to a standstill because of the bombing of their cities. Our job in the Royal Observer Corps now became very boring after the eighteen months blitzing, and I wanted action. At the commencement of the war I had applied for release to join the RAF but this was promptly refused. I was a full-time Observer, and had had years more experience than any of the others – in fact since 1935 – so I had to stay put. But this non-activity was getting me down. In 1941 Ruth's ARP for animals was also at a standstill, and she wanted to join the WAAF – she hardly ever saw me anyway, so why not? I had my doubts though because she had never been a healthy girl, and I doubted if she would be accepted with her health record. However, she applied and was accepted as physically A1.

Early in 1942 Ruth was stationed at Bridlington in Yorkshire, billeted in unfinished, very damp, houses which were not improving her health. I had time off, and spent a few days in Bridlington. I asked Ruth's officer in charge if she could be transferred closer to home, but was refused. However, the officer in charge was more reasonable when I mentioned my friend Group-Captain Broadhurst in

Hornchurch. Within six weeks Ruth was posted to Debden in Essex – it is surprising what can be achieved by 'pulling rank'.

In June 1942 I discussed my possible transfer from the Royal Observer Corps into the Royal Air Force, with Group-Captain Broadhurst and, as my own organisation would not release me, he gave me a note to one of his friends at Adastral House saying that once I had signed on in the RAF the Royal Observer Corps could do nothing about it.

I entered the Royal Air Force on 22 June 1942 as a very second class airman, arriving at Cardington for kitting out and posting. We went through the usual process of medical checks and injections – and I was astounded to see chaps half as big again as me keel over and collapse at the sight of a needle, long before the injection. Clothing was a bit hit and miss – the stores person looked us over, threw a bundle at us saying that will do. However we got the right size boots and forage cap. The uniform turned out to be a near miss, but it had to do. This kitting out was a two day process, then we looked out for where we were going to be posted. In this early preamble I was asked about my background, schooling and general education, and what branch of the Service I would like to muster to. I said I had belonged to a flying club before the war and the Royal Observer Corps up to the time of entry. So, would I be air crew? My papers were looked for and could not be found. Then I was asked more questions and because of my age I was told I was too old for operational flying. And so I passed on with no idea of what the future was to hold. All of my batch of recruits were posted and a new lot had come in, but I was still there. I asked why this was and was promptly told to shut up, and that I would find out in due course. I spent three weeks in that horrible place peeling potatoes and cleaning out latrines. Then my papers finally arrived, but I was still not told what branch of the Service I would be mustered into or posted to. Then we were put on a train and taken north. The first stop was Boston in Lincolnshire where those in the rear of the train were told to disembark, together with myself and one other from the front of the train.

We were marched round the town of Boston and the corporal in charge knocked at doors to see who would take in some of his 'flock'. It rather reminded me of the slave days of selling to the highest bidder. We covered a considerable mileage with fifty 'bodies' to dispose of, and I was the last to be housed, finding myself billeted with a delightful couple with a six year old daughter. They made me and my companion feel so very welcome, as though we were indeed part of the family and that friendship has lasted forty-seven years.

We did our 'square bashing' in some of the side streets without disrupting too much traffic and local life. On our second morning parade we heard the sad news that our other colleagues, who were going on to Skegness, had all been killed or badly maimed in a bombing raid. Again I had missed death, by being removed from that part of the train – so there must have been a good reason somewhere for this.

With the exception of this unfortunate incident our eight weeks' stay at Boston was not very eventful. The tedium of our daily routine of drill and marching was compensated by the comfort and pleasure of our digs. It really was home from home. We could come and go as we pleased whether or not our hosts were home, trusting us completely from the first day. And it was during this time at Boston that news came through that I was being posted to the Central Link Training School at Elstree in Hertfordshire.

The Link Trainer was a simulator for teaching pilots to fly on instruments only, without any external visual aids. The cockpit was similar to that in the actual aircraft but, when the hood was closed, the pilot had nothing but the instruments to fly by. Wind speeds and direction, turbulence and all the normal conditions in flying, were simulated and controlled by the instructor. Linked to the simulator was an instrument known as 'the crab'. This would travel the actual route the pilot was flying on a chart which would show any deviation from the course given by the instructor, whether correct compass settings were made to compensate for drift created by cross winds, and estimated time of arrival allowing for head or following winds, having been given their velocity.

I spent three months at the school with forty hours of lectures covering theory of flight, navigation, instrument panels, maintenance, senior flying training school controlled approach, operational training unit controlled approach, beam approach and landing, descent through cloud, beam approach bleep signals, fighter operational unit procedure and station requirements. During this period I had three weeks at No 1 Elementary Flying Training School in Hatfield doing twelve hours' instrument flying in Proctor aircraft.

During my stay at Elstree I did fifty hours' Link Trainer flying. And on 15 December 1942 I was posted to No 16 OTU (Operational Training Unit) at Upper Heyford in Oxfordshire as an Instructor. During the first two weeks instructing here I put in 103 hours, with three days off at Christmas. We qualified as Instructors with the rank of sergeant, which I felt made up a little for my miserable three weeks at Cardington. Our unit comprised of an officer and four sergeants. Our work was primarily with pilots who were here for their final training before going on operations in bombers. There were a few exceptions with aircrew who had already done one tour of operations and were acting as instructors before doing a second tour. The non-operational pilots took a dim view of we Link types and our infernal machines and, although they had to do their Link training, many did it with very poor grace. It was not until they had done a few sticky operations that they appreciated its value.

We had a satellite aerodrome at a charming place called Hinton-in-the-Hedges, and I was posted out there for three months. The village had one pub and a small store, but the most popular venue was a WVS canteen – a little hut in the centre of the main street. The village comprised some quite stately homes, and a number of the well-to-do ladies from these homes worked in the WVS hut, and because I got on extremely well with them, for several evenings in the week I would be invited to one of their sumptuous homes to dinner.

April 1943 saw me reluctantly back at Heyford dining in the Sergeants' mess. In August I had to return to CLTS Elstree and was upgraded to Senior Instructor, implementing somewhat more sophisticated training procedures because bombing raids had built up and new techniques were being introduced. September saw me at another satellite – this time at Barford – right out in the wilds. As it looked as though I would be there for some time I got permission to live out. Ruth had been ill, and invalided out of the WAAF, and we were able to get digs at a farm near the satellite. We had three very pleasant months here together, and her health did improve a bit. Then I went back to Heyford, and another trip to CLTS for further upgrading. Back at Heyford a new runway was being constructed, so all flying was being done from the satellites. My Link CO decided he and I would stay at Heyford, and the other instructors go to the satellites. After a couple of days he decided to 'get lost'. A week later he returned, and suggested I did the same. We continued this arrangement for five to six weeks until flying returned to Heyford.

The signal now came through that I should put in for a commission. I had my medical and interview, and was posted to 12 base Binbrook – a Lancaster operational base from which 100 Squadron was operating – to await further instructions. During my six weeks' stay here my affection for the Lancaster bomber grew stronger, together with the crews who flew in them, saddened at times though by the inevitable non-return of some of the less fortunate.

During these war years I developed a love of three aircraft in particular. The first was the Spitfire for its grace and performance demonstrated so well during the Battle of Britain. The second was the Wellington bomber for its geodetic construction giving it remarkable strength – I remember one returning to Binbrook from a bombing raid with a huge hole blown in its fuselage that a small car could have been driven through, yet it still survived the journey back from Germany. And the third was that grand old lady the Lancaster that handled well and did such stalwart work towards Britain's survival.

From Binbrook I was posted to the Officers' School at Cosford, where I injured my back three-quarters of the way through the assault course, preventing me from finishing the course. After four weeks' sick treatment I was posted to North Luffenham in Rutland to the Heavy Glider Conversion Unit. But before I had settled in – three weeks in fact – the whole Unit was moved to Brize Norton in Oxfordshire. This transfer to Brize Norton called for a party before departure. We had our party and on the morning of departure, my co-pilot turned up looking awful. This was to be my first time in a Horsa glider and my co-pilot said I would have to fly it. We hooked on behind an old Whitley bomber which was to be our tug and, finally, off we trundled, with several tons of equipment on board and we were almost at the end of the runway before we got airborne. All went well until we were suddenly tossed about the sky like a leaf in a storm. No one had told me that the most important thing when being towed is to keep out of the slipstream of the tug. I really had to fight to keep control, and my co-pilot, having been shaken back to consciousness, then told me what the trouble was, and we continued the journey without further incident. It is a lovely feeling to be up in the air without the roar of engines, particularly when the towing hawser is released. There is just the sound of the wind, and you have a wonderful feeling of detachment from the material world for a short while.

We had only been at Brize Norton for three days when I had an SOS from home. When Ruth had been discharged from the WAAF on medical grounds it was because of arthritis and lung trouble. And now her lungs had become worse and the situation was getting critical. I was given leave to go home and see exactly what the position was. I met the consultant whose verdict was anything but reassuring. Ruth had bronchiectasis and her lungs were in a chronic state. If she could go to Switzerland or Canada, she might possibly survive five years at most but, here in England her chances were very small. If she kept out of all dust by wearing a mask, avoiding anything strenuous, she might survive for twelve months. It was ironic that there was Hitler 'knocking hell' out of London, Ruth was in the middle of it, and the consultant was talking of avoiding dust!

Our own doctor promised to do all he could for Ruth, and to keep me and my CO posted with news. After three lots of compassionate leave I was posted to 21 EFTS (Elementary Flying Training School) at Booker, near High Wycombe, from where I could get home more easily, if necessary. And it was just about now that a very remarkable thing happened. Something that, unbeknown to us at that time, was to change the whole course of our lives.

4

MIRACLES AND MEDIUMSHIP

Ruth was out one day when she met an old friend whom she had not seen for many years. When this lady saw her she asked Ruth what was wrong with her because she looked so ill. Ruth told her briefly what the situation was, which was this: in addition to the lung problem she had developed a mastoid which, if not operated on within ten days, would result in meningitis (for which, at that time, there was no cure). They could not, however, operate because the lungs would not survive the anaesthetic, so it looked like she was going to die one way or the other, pretty soon. (Ruth only told me about the mastoid much later because she had not wanted to worry me.)

Ruth's friend ('Auntie Snell' as she was affectionately called) suggested that Ruth accompany her to her church to meet the healer. Ruth was a bit sceptical but discussed it with her brother who said she had nothing to lose, so the next Monday Auntie Snell called for Ruth and took her to a Spiritualist church. This did not bother Ruth because, what with her difficulty with breathing, perpetual coughing, earache and sickness, she had lost interest in practically everything.

Particulars having been taken, Ruth was ushered into the healing room, to be met by Mrs Eva Rayner, the leader of the church and principal healer. She wore a white coat and, when she spoke, Ruth thought her voice was deep for a woman. Mrs Rayner told Ruth that she was going to perform a psychic operation on her ear. She worked on the mastoid bone for two minutes and then said that Ruth would have no further trouble with it. At this point Mrs Rayner, who now sounded like a man, explained that it was really Dr Lewis from the realm of spirit working through her, his medium. Mrs Rayner/Dr Lewis said that to treat Ruth's lungs was going to be more difficult but, they could be helped if Ruth attended regularly for healing. The healer also suggested that Ruth should show her doctor her ear, and enjoy his surprise when he sees it.

Next day Ruth went to see the doctor, and when he examined the ear he said he was amazed because it was chronic two days before and now was perfectly healthy. There was no sign of disease.

The weekend after this remarkable happening I was home – since my posting to Booker I was able to get home each weekend. Ruth told me what had happened and I was so astonished that I quite forgot to be angry with her for not telling me the seriousness of it the weekend before.

Having gone into the RAF to get some action, I had spent two years – with the exception of Binbrook – in isolated areas of the country on training stations, far removed from hostilities, so you will readily appreciate my going home to London at weekends was a two edged sword – going home to a very sick wife and to having to brave the German doodle bugs and rockets.

I recall, one evening we had been visiting my parents, and Ruth was living with hers close by. We were just going over the railway bridge remembered from our young day antics, when there was an almighty explosion and flash. I threw Ruth to the ground and fell on top of her and, as I did so, it was as though all the air had been sucked out of my lungs. We got shakily to our feet and on getting to her parents' home we found the rocket had landed on the railway station, and a section of railway line had been flung several hundred yards and gone through a solid oak door of the church opposite their flat. All the windows of the flat were broken and her father, who had been bedridden for twelve months, had been hurled into the air, bed and all. Talking about it later Ruth said, 'It's the doodle bugs we hated most – you heard the engine cut, counting the seconds before the explosion, never knowing quite where it was going to be. With the rockets – if you were alive to hear the explosion, you would have a pretty good chance of survival.'

After six months of regular healing Ruth's health had

improved to such an extent that the doctor suggested some kind of occupation would be good for her, provided it was not too strenuous. I suggested we should have a go at toy making. Toys were in short supply with the war on, so I started making a few enquiries about possible material supplies. Ruth was in Palmers Green, and not too far away in Edmonton, there were a number of firms making shoes and slippers. I wrote to them asking if I could have their off-cuts of felt and velvet from the slippers. These firms replied that we could take away what we wanted when they knew what it was for, so we were set up for materials. Now I had to get down to making some patterns. First on the list were balls made in different coloured segments. They looked quite attractive and we decided on three different sizes ranging from three to nine inches in diameter. We made up half a dozen of each size, and Ruth went round the local shops to see what sales were likely to be. They went in twos and threes, and then one shop suggested that we make some animals, as they are always popular. So, we branched out with a rabbit, a cat and a teddy bear. The turnover was a steady trickle, just enough to keep Ruth occupied.

I suppose it is inevitable that one becomes a bit ambitious with something that one enjoys and, having a drink with my father one Saturday evening, I was talking about our little project saying that it did not look as though it would grow very much unless we could get sales further afield. He thought for a minute, and then said that he had a friend who was in the toy wholesale business and that he would speak to him for us. Next weekend my father rang me to say that he had had a word with John Levy about the toys, and he wanted to see some samples. I took him a sample range to see what he could do. He said to contact him the following weekend, and he would let me know if any of his contacts were interested. When I phoned the following week I had a terrific shock when he said that he wanted 100 gross of each of the three sizes of coloured balls which was $100 \times 144 \times 3 = 43,200$. We could make a dozen a day but these were required within six weeks. When I told Ruth she was equally amazed. We shut ourselves away to do our sums and, after a couple of hours, decided that if we could recruit about twenty-five helpers we might actually get somewhere near the deadline. And we decided we would have a go. Next morning I phoned the factories to make sure no one else would have any offcuts for the next few weeks, then set off with two large expanding suitcases to collect my spoils, while Ruth went round all her friends to see how many she could persuade to help to sew these many splendoured things. I did two trips to the factories that morning, and Ruth got eight or nine promises of help, so we thought we had got off to a fair start. And when I got back to camp I would have a recruiting drive in the village to see how many women wanted to earn some extra pocket money machining.

We spent Saturday afternoon and evening, and Sunday until five o'clock in the afternoon cutting out segments ready for sewing. I went back to camp with one suitcase full of cut segments ready for sewing (in the hope that I could find people to do them) and the other suitcase full of offcuts to cut out in my spare time. I had a groove in my thumb about a quarter of an inch deep from the scissors and two days of cutting felt and velvet.

I averaged six hours a day instruction at Booker, leaving the evenings reasonably free to go on my recruiting drive for home machinists. One of the Station Firemen was very helpful. He lived locally, knew everyone and, in no time at all, had a dozen or so willing workers lined up for me.

Halfway through our six weeks' time schedule it was beginning to look quite promising, giving us more heart to press on. Each weekend was a repetition of the first, one mad rush from start to finish, with one additional function now, filling and finishing off the balls. By now my in-laws' flat was full of them. They had completely taken over until we were able to persuade the wholesalers to take a load away. The sixth week was rather like an extended madhouse, both at home and on camp. I had even got some of the lads busy stuffing until I realised I would not be able to get them home because of the bulk. Again my fireman friend came to the rescue. He had a car, and offered transport. We worked on well into Saturday night, and Sunday at 10.30 pm the last box was packed, and sealed, ready for collection next day. We had achieved what had seemed impossible. Then I had to get back to Booker, and finished up by borrowing a bicycle and cycling for three and a half hours in the early hours of the morning. But I didn't care – we were in business, and enjoying the challenge.

It was June, 1945 and, with the exception of the Japanese, the war was as good as over. We had a lot of Canadians on the camp waiting their demobilisation, and they were a real crazy bunch. The evenings in the Sergeants' mess would develop into a steeple chase on RAF bikes. The trestle tables were arranged one central table standing normally with one on either side, with the outside legs folded in, so that they rode up the slope of one on to the level one, and down the other side. These would be arranged all round the mess, and they would set off at brief intervals going in opposite directions!! I leave the rest to your imagination – it was chaotic to say the least.

I first went to Booker on 1 December 1944 and, as the camp was very isolated, we would often go into Marlow in the evening to a nice little pub by the river. One evening we had been discussing the possibility of putting on a pantomime on the camp, and agreed it would be a good idea. I didn't remember next day, but it seemed I'd agreed to be Red Riding Hood and I had, incidentally, grown an eight inch 'Flying Officer Kite' moustache by now. Anyway, rehearsals went ahead, and the big night arrived. I was to make a spectacular aerial entry on a rope!! I was on top of a crate in the wings waiting to 'take off' in full kit, with everything they could lay their hands on attached, pots, pans, mugs, the lot. Off I went in a graceful(?) swallow dive which should have taken me across the stage. But, oh no! The twit who fixed the rope made it too long, and I belly flopped in the middle of the stage, skinning both knees! But the show must go on, and it did. It was, of course, a skit on the real thing, and proved a great success. Thereafter, if the CO wanted me he would say 'Tell that Link chap what's his name? You know, Red Riding Hood, I want to see him.' With the stress of our business project, I had become increasingly aware of my old back injury from the assault course. I do not know whether this had been caused by carrying heavy cases about, or was the effect of six very stressful weeks but I had a week's leave, went home, saw my doctor who ordered a complete rest. He wrote a note which we sent to my CO prolonging my leave at home but, after two weeks, the powers that be decreed I should be in an RAF hospital, and I was transported in a jeep ten miles to Great Portland Street. This journey was agony and then when

I arrived it was decided to give me deep massage on my spine which made it infinitely worse. Not only was the pain intensified, but my back was now in spasm. I thought I was developing St Vitus Dance. I reported this latest development and, as a result, was sent to see a psychiatrist who spent two hours trying to persuade me to admit that I was skiving, and trying to get out of the Service. Then, having decided that nothing could be done for me, I was sent back to camp. Reporting to the CO, he was surprised at my condition – I could not stand upright, my back was constantly twitching, and I was in pain from head to feet. I had a pocket full of painkillers, but they did little to help. My CO agreed that I was in no fit state to work so he told me to go home while he arranged for my release from the RAF.

During these months of misery Ruth had repeatedly tried to get me to have healing from the church that had been her saviour, but I had convinced myself that it would not benefit me. I thought that she was a much more spiritual person than me and that was why she had been healed in that remarkable way. However, having reached a stage of feeling that I had had as much as I can take of being half-paralysed, never out of pain, and seriously looking to a way of ending it all, I felt an unusual inner compulsion to go to the church with Ruth one Sunday. I tried to fight against it, but could not get away from the feeling that I had to go. Needless to say, she was delighted having tried to persuade me for so long. I did not quite know what to expect when the service started, everything seemed perfectly normal – prayers, hymns, readings from the Bible, except that the prayers were not read from a book, or repeated as is so often the case with no voice modulation or feeling. These prayers were voiced from the heart and held one's attention. You listened because they meant something. Then came the address – I had been brought up on Anglican sermons that people tend to fall asleep in – but this was different. It was given by the leader of the church and I was fascinated. Her eyes were tightly closed yet she moved about the rostrum with complete ease and confidence as though she had her eyes wide open. I thought of our childhood days playing 'blind man's buff' when, within seconds, you have lost all sense of bearing and direction. Ruth whispered, 'It's Dr Lewis, she's in trance.' I liked the address because we were being 'talked to' not 'talked at', and it sounded good common sense. But I was still intrigued by the ease with which she moved about avoiding obstacles. At the end of the service Ruth said that there would be clairvoyance where the medium brings messages from people who have gone over to the next life. The medium stood up, this time not in trance, looked around and pointing at me said, 'I want to come to you sir'. I wished the floor would open and swallow me. But the medium continued, 'I have someone by the name of Ginger wishing to contact you – can you place him?' I couldn't place him and she was silent for a few moments then said, 'Ah! he's telling me to remind you of a tram.' This was the tram we had blown off the track as choir boys. What fantastic proof of survival after death. No one, other than we two, ever knew of that incident and our involvement. We had been too scared to breath a word to anyone – even Ruth did not know. The medium then said that I should attend for healing.

I thought afterwards that the medium had been spot on about Ginger and the tram, and must therefore know what she was talking about. I duly went for healing next day expecting my spine to be worked on, but as soon as I was on the healing couch, the medium pointed out that I was having problems with my feet. This was true as I suffered very badly with athlete's foot. And in three days they were perfect – I just could not believe such a transformation was possible. However, my back did not change. I attended every Monday for about six weeks without any noticeable change, going through the day with perpetual dull pain all over my body, fitful sleep, waking to another day of nagging discomfort. Until I woke one morning to no pain. I wriggled about – still no pain – got out of bed and realised I was free from pain. I very gently moved my back, bent forward and backward, and still all right. This really was fantastic and no mistake. Medically relegated to a wheelchair, here I was, back to a normal human being again.

But how are these wonders performed? I needed to know about these astonishing powers that made the seemingly impossible, possible, and an intelligence superior to our physical understanding. I asked Mrs Rayner if I might be allowed to join one of the developing groups to see if I had any potential at all. She replied that Dr Lewis had been waiting for me and so we entered into the most interesting study of ourselves, and another aspect of life I had never dreamed of. Ruth was taken into an afternoon group and I joined an evening one, and we appreciated how fortunate we were, because there was always a waiting list of people waiting to get into them.

During my incapacity the toy business had been sadly neglected, and it was necessary for me to earn a living. And then an opportunity seemed to fall into my lap. I went into a wholesale electrical company to enquire the whereabouts of a certain firm, and got into conversation with a man who turned out to be the boss. In conversation it came out that I was looking for a sales representative's job, preferably in the motor trade. I saw this man's eyes light up a bit, and he said, 'What about the auto-electrical trade?' I said that that would be all right and he revealed that he wanted a sales representative for North London and Essex. We spent the rest of the afternoon going through their huge stock of all items needed to repair any electrical equipment on cars and commercial vehicles. There were several hundred different parts to deal with. I made myself a sample case with front, sides and top, all hinged so that it opened up and laid flat, lined it with felt, and had a large selection of these components fixed to it. In this way customers could see at a glance what they wanted without having to thumb through catalogues. This went down well, and soon my sales topped those of the senior representative. He got niggled, fell out with the boss, who suggested he copied my example with a display case. After a further two rows he left and I was made sales manager, and life began to flow smoothly again.

Week after week I sat in the group trying, as we were told, to raise our consciousness to the highest level, shutting out thoughts of the everyday material aspect of our lives. But I found this impossible – every imaginable stupid thought would persist in flitting in and out of my mind until I got quite exasperated. One by one the other group members would make progress, either with clairvoyance, clairaudience or trance speaking, but nothing happened for me.

During this time a friend had found us a house in Winchmore Hill, and Mrs Rayner had asked us to take in a young church member to help him find his own feet. Fraser had lived with his mother who had made such a fuss of him that he could not do anything for himself. We were in the same developing group together too.

At last this period of sitting with nothing happening came to an end. I felt a strong urge to stand up and speak. I got to my feet and apparently at the same time Fraser also stood up, his control bowed, and he sat down until I had finished speaking. I was not aware of this until told afterwards. This was my first contact with Spirit that I was aware of. We had opened the door at last, and could do this at home too. My contact was a North American Indian giving the name of White Eagle, Ruth's was Sister Frances and Fraser's The Pilgrim. We had been taught the importance of prayer for protection and to raise our consciousness as high as possible to avoid interference from the lower astral levels in spirit. When we sat at home we would take it in turns to give the opening and closing prayers at the start and finish of our sessions. We felt very privileged to belong to this excellent teaching centre – 'The Temple of the Trinity' in Palmers Green, North London. It was a hard school, but developed some first class mediums and healers.

No one was allowed to take the rostrum, or platform, until they were sufficiently well trained in correct presentation, dress, delivery, interpretation of spirit messages and speech. Some had to attend speech training classes until their speaking was considered good enough for platform work.

It was a good year since I had started trance speaking in the group when I was told that I would take the service on the following Sunday. As a youngster I had been on the shy side, and this was something I had not bargained for – speaking in front of a crowd of people. The thought scared me to death, but I was assured that everything would be all right, and I would get plenty of support from the congregation.

I spent quite a long time on Saturday writing out the theme of the talk I was to give the next day – read it through several times until I had got the general gist of it fairly well in my mind, and I felt a bit easier as a result. So when the moment came I stood up knowing what I was going to talk about until after a short while, I could hear my voice talking about a completely different subject. It was a strange experience, hearing my voice in the distance as though it belonged to someone else. One thing it did teach me though was never to make notes, or prepare for a talk – our controls are doing the talking, not us.

At about the same time that I took the platform, so did Fraser for speaking, and Ruth for clairvoyance – in fact, we seemed to work so much together that Dr Lewis referred to us as 'my three'. One service we always looked forward to was Holy Communion. This was once a month and, although Mrs Rayner was in deep trance with eyes closed, Dr Lewis knew each communicant by name, and had a personal message for each one – usually about our own development, but always pertinent to the individual.

The developing groups were run in a series of threes. One week Dr Lewis would talk to us, the next week we would be invited to question him on any subject that had bearing on our spiritual understanding and development, and the third would be for our own development when, during meditation and attunement we would be encouraged to voice anything that came into our mind or spiritual vision.

As the years went by this really became our spiritual home, and we would miss nothing that went on there. We even came back off holiday so as not to miss a group or service. There was a need for other outlets, however, and this was encouraged. One of the members was very gifted and produced two spiritual plays – *Romeo and Juliet* in both this world and spirit, and *The Voice from Spirit* – two excellent productions that received much acclaim and were, in fact, put on in London, with considerable success. On the lighter side we ran a concert party – we called ourselves 'The Reprobates', and put on a number of good shows from time to time.

At this time I was still travelling with my job, and covered the whole of London and East Anglia. My part in The Reprobates was basically comedy, and I had a number of amusing sketches which literally 'came to me from out of the blue'. Driving along, a thought would come into my mind and, in no time at all, I had developed a sketch which I found I could retain, word for word, for hours until I had time to put it on paper. When this happened the second time I realised it was the patter and style of the late Tommy Handley, being given to me in a way that I could never have done by myself.

During this time my own work as sales manager for the wholesalers' auto-electrical components company had built up very well, and we had renewed contact with the toy wholesalers who had started us off with the initial order for Woolworths. We had made considerable progress, and now had a range of teddy bears and other animals made out of genuine sheepskin, dyed in various colours. These were being supplied to stores such as Hamleys and Harrods, via the wholesalers, and we now employed three girls on a full-time basis, to cope with the steady weekly turnover. Our front room at home had been converted into a workroom, with a cutting table, machines and bales of kapok, one girl doing the cutting, one machining, and the other stuffing. Ruth would do the faces of the animals and finishing off.

We submitted a complete range of toys to be shown at the British Industries Fair, and went on the stand of our wholesalers to see the reaction of the trade to our products. We had registered our name of 'D-Lite Toys', displayed a range of six sizes of teddy bear from six inches to four feet tall – all, with the exception of the smallest, having moving head, arms and legs. We also produced rabbits in pastel colours and the balls were still popular in some areas, also cats and a terrier dog on wheels that a child could ride on, pull or push along. I had designed all of the toys.

5

PHYSICAL MEDIUMSHIP

Our doctor, with whom we were friendly, knew of our interest in the spiritual world because of our healing. One day when we met he told me that his wife was psychic and suggested that Ruth and I join them in a seance. We agreed and a week or two later they came round to our house for the evening. It was a cold winter night and we had a nice welcoming fire ready for them. We had a round heavy oak table, about three feet in diameter, which we put near the fireplace, and the four of us sat round it. The doctor's wife took over the proceedings and told us to rest our hands on top of the table and ask if there was any spirit contact there. If there was, then the table would move. This we did and, sure enough, the table rocked from side to side. We asked several questions to which the table would lift one side – once for a negative answer, and twice for a positive one. Ruth made some laughing comment to one of their answers, and the table immediately turned over on its side into the hearth with the top only a foot away from the flames. We tried to pick it up, but it would not budge. It was as though it was fastened to the floor. Ruth was told that it would not move unless she apologised, which she thought was ridiculous. However, the table was getting very hot and still we could not move it, so Ruth apologised and the table righted itself.

We finished our seance and agreed to meet again the following Saturday evening. This time the doctor's wife stayed away from the table, leaving we three to see what we could produce. Things went along quite well for a while until the table started to develop some peculiar antics. It started rocking violently against me, hitting me in the stomach, gradually forcing me across the room until I was pinned in a corner. I was really scared by this and could do nothing. The doctor called to his wife to stop it and, to my great relief, it did stop. We then discovered she was a very powerful psychic, and she thought the whole incident quite funny.

Next day was Sunday and we went to church as usual and, after the service Mrs Rayner sent a message out to us to say that Dr Lewis wanted to talk to us. She reported to us that Dr Lewis knew we had been up to something and that we should stop it immediately. We had got ourselves involved with some evil influences that they had great difficulty in controlling. We said what had happened and were told to have nothing to do with them again – the doctor's wife was linked with undesirable forces. Frankly, this warning was not really necessary – I was far too scared to repeat the experience. But it showed, yet again, just how much care and concern our spirit friends had for us, and the close association established between the two worlds.

At the Temple of the Trinity there was a small 'closed circle' for psychic phenomena, with a few sitters chosen by Dr Lewis, who met regularly with a physical medium. After our unpleasant experience at home, we were invited to join this closed circle. It was looked upon as an honour to be part of it, but we did not need any physical proof of the continuity of life after physical death – we had had adequate proof ourselves, but there were obviously other reasons for our being there. In those early days of psychic phenomena this kind of mediumship was deemed necessary to prove to the disbelievers the reality of these unseen energies, and intelligences, that could produce such amazing results. Let me share some of them with you.

John, our medium, was a strapping well-built young man who, like many other wartime flyers, had become aware of unusual reactions when away from earth conditions – a feeling of detachment from materialism and an awareness of something finer, the awakening of his psychic, or spiritual, awareness. As an RAF pilot he did not have too much time to study these odd feelings, but, after the war, together with some of his friends, he realised he had this ability to be used for actual physical manifestations.

The Temple had originally been a bank, and the seance

room had been the strongroom having reinforced concrete walls and steel door. One corner opposite the door was curtained off, behind which the medium sat. We sat around the room, Mrs Rayner on one side of the curtain, and me on the other with the other sitters spaced round between. In one corner was one of the old type of wind-up gramophones and a pile of '78' records. At the commencement of the seance the main light would be switched off leaving just a soft red light. A prayer would be said, and a record softly played. After a minute or two we heard a sharp swish as the curtain was whipped open, followed by a thud, and there was John sitting in the centre of the room. All of this took a split second. John was in a deep trance as though he and the chair were one inseparable unit. Then we watched a substance issuing from his nose and mouth, flowing down like a very fine gossamer cobweb, spreading out until it covered the whole of the front of his body, extending to the floor. This remained for about a minute, and then slowly withdrew back into his body through the nose and mouth from whence it had come. This substance is called ectoplasm, and is used by spirit to create all manner of physical manifestations.

Then we may have 'direct voice' phenomena, where a voice box would be built up with ectoplasm, away from the medium, and discarnate souls would speak to us in their own voices. We were privileged to converse with my father, Ruth's father, and others that we had been close to before they passed on to this higher life, and there was no doubting their voices. The medium had never met any of them at any time, so there was no question of fraudulence on his part, as was sometimes said of some physical mediums.

On another occasion we saw the ectoplasm manifesting, but this time it was in the form of a rod, or tube, about a quarter of an inch in diameter. We watched this rod move across the floor to the corner where the gramophone was, and then, to our amazement, it picked up this fairly heavy instrument, and it was swung around over our heads still playing, without any interruption, finally putting it down exactly where it had picked it up. It then picked up the stack of '78' records, which really were heavy, and they too circled over our heads several times before being returned to the table once more. The rod was then withdrawn into the body of the medium.

Sometimes we would have an aport, which is when an object dematerialises from outside the seance room and rematerialises again inside. We had a brass figure of Christ taken from a drawer in the vestry, and dropped on the floor in front of us. Flowers would be taken off the altar and put into our lap, the stems still wet from the vase they had been taken from. The room was always checked before a seance, as was John, our medium. The walls were concrete, the door solid steel which was locked with a sitter sitting back to it, so there was no way any object could have got in other than being dematerialised and rematerialised.

There were times when discarnate souls would materialise in their physical form. Ruth's father materialised on one occasion, talked to us, and just as additional proof of his identity, bent his head forward right in front of our faces saying, 'You see, I still have my good head of hair' – this was something he had always been proud of, right up to his passing, a thick head of wavy, iron grey hair.

On another occasion a huge black Negro figure built up at least seven feet tall, beautifully muscled and clad in just a loincloth. He stood there for a few moments then, raising his arms, thumped his chest to prove how solid he was, and this was just the same as any living being would have sounded doing the same. Then his voice boomed out, 'Me Wapella, me doorkeeper,' then slowly the figure melted away. He was responsible for seeing that no unwanted spirit people intruded the circles.

The one experience that has meant most to us, and is as vivid and real today as it was then thirty-five years ago, was the materialisation of our daughter, Susan. In 1944 Ruth had lost a baby with a late miscarriage, and we had been told in the group that she was being looked after by my paternal grandmother. But this experience we had never dreamed of. Her little soft, warm hand caressing our faces so lovingly, then turning to me said, 'I'm not like you Daddy, I'm like Mummy, I've got blue eyes and fair hair, but I do love you.' This was our daughter growing up in spirit into a beautiful child.

We questioned Dr Lewis about children passing over, and whether we stay the same as when we die? He said that a child will grow to what we on earth call the 'prime of life', and elderly people will return to that same level although often, if they come back to us to identify themselves, and reassure us that they are still very much alive, they will come back as we last saw them making the recognition easier.

We have had the privilege of watching Susan grow up into womanhood, a very beautiful, knowledgeable, spiritual soul, who has now been attached to her mother's group of helpers for a number of years.

The medium was under the control of an Egyptian, El Rashed, who would open the seance after the little cockney boy, Johnny, had got the vibration of the circle up with his particular cockney humour. El Rashed was a great poet, and it was a delight to listen to his wonderful flow of words that always had a sound spiritual message.

Levitation can be an interesting experience too. On one occasion when John was sitting in the chair entranced, Mrs Rayner and I were told to each take one of his hands. We did and, almost immediately, the chair with John sitting in it rose up until we had to stand to retain a hold on his hands. Then the chair tilted forward until its back was resting on the ceiling. John was still sitting in his normal position, but now facing down on us. No normal material power could have held him in this position unless he was strapped in, which he certainly was not. Then the back of the chair came down returning to its normal upright position and lowered once more to the floor.

Sometimes trumpets would be used to convey messages to the sitters by direct voice, using ectoplasm once more to direct the trumpet.

One of the highlights of the year was the Christmas party for the spirit children. This was held in the main body of the church. There was one large Xmas tree decorated with lots of toys both on the tree, and underneath. The church was blacked out, and again John was our medium. As soon as he was in trance we heard the sound of toys being taken off the tree among squeals of delight from the spirit children. Toys could be heard skating across the floor, and this went on for about an hour. At the end of the session and the lights turned on, the tree wa stripped bare, and toys were all over the place. They really had enjoyed themselves.

A few months after I started platform speaking I had some extraordinary experiences. I was still travelling for the electrical components firm, which took me all over the country. Twice a year I would go to Scotland for two weeks and, on one of these visits, I was telling a customer in Edinburgh that I would be staying there over the weekend. He invited me to spend Sunday with him and his family in their small crofter's cottage. I thanked him and agreed to visit – and while I was there he told me about his three-year-old daughter who had been born physically disabled, and in spite of numerous operations, still could not walk. She was due to return to hospital the following week for yet more surgery. After dinner we sat again relaxing and chatting when a door opened in the living room and a child tottered in, came over to me holding out her arms to be picked up. I put her on my knee and, turning to the parents said, 'I didn't know you had another daughter.' Then I saw the look of amazement on their faces. This was not another daughter, but the child who had never walked by herself before. I had never seen her before, but found it hard to believe this was the same child that they had told me about an hour or two earlier. We all agreed this was indeed a miracle because she looked so healthy now too. She stayed up with us for several hours playing with her toys, and it was a most fascinating experience that I will never forget. They promised they would let me know the outcome of the following week's surgery. I spoke to several people about the remarkable incident, and, like me, they found it hard to believe.

On my return home a week later a letter awaited me from the child's parents. They had taken her to hospital, but the consultant would not accept it was the same child he had operated on nine times until he saw the scars from the previous operations. He was dumbfounded, called in another consultant, and they could not find anything physically wrong with her. The parents were absolutely over the moon about it.

A few days later I met a friend who told me that my old friend Bill, with whom I had shared some hair raising experiences in the Observer Corps, was very ill in Oldchurch Hospital, Romford, and not expected to live. So I made it my business to visit him as soon as I could. On arrival, I told the

Ward Sister I wanted to see Mr Comber, but was told that this would not be possible because he had been in a coma for a week and was unlikely to recover. I explained that I had travelled a long way and would just like to have a peep for a minute or two. The Ward Sister reluctantly agreed, and so I sat by his bedside feeling sorry that our long pleasureable association was coming to a close. I rested my hand lightly on the bed covers in a sort of farewell gesture. After a few moments he moved, opened his eyes, recognised me and smiled. Within minutes he was sitting up recounting some of our wartime experiences. The Ward Sister came in and was amazed, and Bill was discharged three days later. I thought this was a strange event but just another of those odd coincidences like the little Scottish girl.

It was three weeks after this incident that I had a call from a friend to say her husband had suffered a severe heart attack, and asked if I would go and see him. When I went into the ward I found him in an oxygen tent. He looked dreadful – his face and hands were blue and he was generally in very poor shape indeed. Sitting at his bedside I felt impelled to slip my hand under the side of the tent, and hold his hand. Gradually his colour began to change to a more normal hue, and he too opened his eyes and wanted to speak. I suggested he should rest and I would call again in a day or two: I left him looking very much better. As I left the ward the Staff Nurse took my arm and asked to have a word with me in her office. She said she had been watching and that it appeared that I had literally brought him back to life. Before my arrival, she had not expected him to survive more than another hour.

The fact of my having any part in these occurrences never entered my head because after Ruth's and my own healing, I thought that anyone involved in healing had to be a very highly evolved individual, which I was certainly not. But, surely, all of these remarkable events could not all be coincidence – there must be a message there somewhere. I spoke to Mrs Rayner of these incidents, and asked if she could explain them. She replied that Dr Lewis wanted to show me that I was needed for healing, and had I been told this without such proof I probably would not have believed him.

It brought home the fact that the basis of all healing is love, compassion and a desire to help alleviate suffering. So I started my healing in the Temple on Monday evenings, and felt very honoured at being elevated to such exalted heights which I had never dreamed of. To me, a healer had been next to God in what I had seen and experienced and, here was I, feeling very humble, realising what I had to live up to and the responsibility.

Twelve months had passed since Ruth's last chest X-ray, and she had to go back to the clinic for further tests. Further X-rays were taken and when the doctor saw them, there was some doubt as to whether they were the correct plates – so more X-rays were taken. This time the doctor knew that these were the correct plates and was amazed that Ruth's lungs were shown as clear – she was cured of an 'incurable' condition. You can imagine how elated we were at this news, and it was not long after this that Mrs Rayner decided to have a service of testimony to healing, and Ruth was one of those chosen to testify to her own healing. However, shortly before the service Dr Lewis said Ruth was not to testify because he said she would never be cured as she had chosen a difficult path in this life, but Spirit would keep her well enough to cope with the problems she had to face, as indeed they were doing now.

As a child she had the hearing in her right ear destroyed by a school doctor who removed (unintentionally) the ear drum. She had continual abscesses in both ears up until the age of eighteen and then several years of monthly visits to St Bartholomew's Hospital for the removal of female polypi from the nose and ears. She had acute sinusitis practically all her life, but in spite of this history the RAF passed her A1 fit on entry into the WAAF during the Second World War. The WAAF were often billeted in wet or damp conditions which, for her, ultimately resulted in severe arthritis and lung trouble. Though they invalided her out with these conditions, they would not accept responsibility for them when she applied for a pension. The RAF's excuse was that these must have been congenital, but had been dormant when Ruth entered the RAF. Finally, there was her entry into the Temple, and Dr Lewis's care for the mastoid and bronchiectasis. At this point she was thirty, and we both wondered what was to come next. I have a great admiration for the way she had dealt with her ill health, always cheerful outwardly – no one meeting her for the first time would ever dream she had been through what she has. I remember going up to St Bartholomew's Hospital with her on one occasion for her regular polypi removal. A young girl in the waiting room was getting very upset at the thought of her own treatment and the doctor reassured her by saying, 'Look at Mrs Anderson, she has it done every month and she doesn't mind'. There were times at home when she would let off steam but, outwardly, she was a wonderful example of how to deal with life generally, and its ups and downs.

I had been a smoker for many years and, as a traveller, it was always looked upon as a friendly gesture to offer a cigarette to a client, and I enjoyed one myself, until one day when I was at my healing session. I had a nasty migraine headache, and a colleague offered to give me healing. I went into his cubicle, he put his hands across my forehead, and I got the most repulsive smell of stale tobacco and nicotine. I opened my eyes and saw the stain on his finger which made me think that if I was repulsed by it, then it must be much worse for a non-smoker. So I gave up smoking from that moment, and found it the easiest thing in the world to do. Other people say it is difficult to give up smoking, but if you have a good enough reason it could not be easier. Every time I thought of smoking I got that awful smell on my colleague's fingers. I also suggested to him that, if he must smoke, to keep his breath and hands clean before healing sessions.

My own business had taken a change now. One of my clients in the West country were repairers and manufacturers of auto-electrical components with two factories, one in Salisbury and one in Yeovil. They wanted to expand their business and had asked me if I would act as their concessionnaire. Ruth and I spent a weekend with them and, having been shown around their works, I decided to accept their offer. This had entailed many changes on my part, as it meant me holding considerable stocks of their products. It was necessary for me to have business premises, and I had been offered three lock-up garages at a nearby petrol station, two of which I used for stock, and the other as an office, with an inter-connecting door through to the stockroom. Once I had established my connections it became largely a mail order business, and clients knowing what I held in stock would telephone their needs, and we would despatch them. After a short while we were despatching four or five heavy mail bags each day. Repeated requests to the post office to collect had always brought the same negative response, which meant I had to take the mail bags to the post office each day. Ruth, who was now in the office and general packer when I was out, could not drive, so I had to be back each day in time to get them away. Business, at this time, 1955, was much easier to lose than gain, and a 'by return' service was essential to retain custom. This was limiting but we managed pretty well.

I was still doing my healing session on Monday evenings when one of the healers died suddenly. After the service on Sunday I was asked if I would take over her Monday afternoon session in addition to my evening one. I said yes, and would start the following day. On the way home I remarked to Ruth that it would mean losing a day's delivery and probably some good customers too. However, the next morning there was a letter from the post office to say that it would now be prepared to collect our mail bags!

Thus some vague sort of pattern was unfolding perhaps that would throw light on why I had survived those earlier mishaps but, what it was, and where it would take us, was as yet quite unpredictable.

After several years' regular attendance in our closed physical circle, John would fail to arrive, and when he did turn up, Johnny, his cockney spirit boy, would materialise a cigarette lighter – neither John, nor any sitter, had one – and run it up and down the curtains. Incidents like this indicated that unwanted influences were creeping in, and we discovered that John was being lured away with offers of high fees by a private group in London's West End. He was given the option of either leaving the private group or ours and, regrettably, the temptation of money got the better of him and he left us. It was not so very long after this that we heard he was ill with severe internal haemorrhaging, no doubt due to interference by a sitter while a physical manifestation was taking place.

Rather than close our circle, it was decided another medium should be trained to carry on and it was decided that it was to be me. One of the women members of the Temple had had a mental breakdown, and when she returned she would punctuate almost every sentence with the phrase 'I do wish I was normal like you.' This, added to the shock of being told I was going to train for physical mediumship, and the remarkable things we had experienced over the last seven or eight years, rather took my breath away, and was responsible for the following odd ode entitled 'My Wish' – which I am sure must have had Tommy Handley behind it.

My Wish

It's me, I'm here, your heart's delight
But Ooh, I've had an awful fright,
'Ere, they said to me one day
We're going to train you in a different way,
We'll see if you've got physical power
Me! a fragile, wilting flower
Then it cut across me like a spasm
They thought I was that chap 'Ector Plasm'
My hair turned white with sudden shock
My eyes popped out like sticks of rock
By the look on their faces I knew it was true
Coo – I didn't half wish I was normal like you

The weeks went by and all seemed bright
I thought they'd forgotten my miserable plight
Then, a touch on the shoulder, they love a jest
Said, Come on old son – we'll give you your test.
They led the way to the seance room door
And my feet did a rat-a-tat-tat on the floor,
No need to be nervous, this should prove quite amusing
That is, if your power supply doesn't start fusing.
I pictured myself stuck up on the ceiling
And being left suspended 'til the next week for healing
I wondered what in the world I would do
Coo – I didn't half wish I was normal like you.

They all trooped in, and then locked the door
I thought this is my lot, and that's for sure,
I was sat in a corner feeling very forlorn
And completely cut off when the curtain was drawn,
Now, take a deep breath, and get down to it son
'Cause I think it's high time this 'ere seance

begun.
The light went out, and they started to sing
And a voice inside me said – Let go of your string!
Well, I reared up like fried bread that was burnt in the pan
And started floating about like a rotating fan.
I was scared to death, hadn't got a clue
Coo – I didn't half wish I was normal like you.

I gazed down at the sitters, some smiling, some glum
And would have sold my soul to be home with my Mum.
Someone, looking up, said – I say, do look there
It's my Auntie Fanny, I can tell by her hair.
Auntie Fanny, my foot – I've seen a few sights
And I think this is one of the Arabian Knights.
They thought this is grand, he's the best of our finds,
I felt more like old Heinz with his 57 kinds.
I wanted to say it was me all the time,
But knew if I did I'd be cut off in my prime.
I felt proper poorly, cold, clammy too,
Coo – I didn't half wish I was normal like you.

Then, one of the sitters, she must have felt gay
Said, Let's have some fun before closing today.
I'll stand over here, and switch on the light
And see if the medium can stay in full flight.
This shattered my dreams 'til I heard someone say
NO. I think that's enough for our first trial day.
Then, someone whispered, I think he's a fraud
What's the betting he's held up by very strong cord.
That hurt my pride, and I started to doubt,
That's when my power supply went up the spout.
I came down with a thud – I thought I'd broken in two
Coo – I didn't half wish I was normal like you.

They gathered me up in a heap by the door,
Then wistfully said, We shan't use him any more.
Then all went quiet, for what seemed like hours,
They was wondering whether to send out for
flowers
When, in comes a big gent, all dressed up in
blue,
Says, Hello, Hello there, what's all this to-do?
What's this great heap of flesh on the floor?
You can't have such rubbish a-blocking the door,
You'd better get rid of it out in the bin
And never, not no how, do this 'ere agin.
That's the end of my story, and some of it's true,
Coo – how I wish I was normal like you.

My development for physical phenomena was different from my trance speaking, in so far as the state of trance was deeper and the seance room was in darkness. With my platform speaking in trance I was vaguely aware of my voice in a disinterested way, rather like someone the other side of the room, holding a conversation with another person. In the seance room I was unaware of my voice, or actions, and seemed to be in a completely different world.

We started with two trumpets for direct voice. These were made of aluminium, with two bands painted round them in phosphorescent paint, so that they would show up in the dark, and a plaque of flat aluminium, eighteen inches by twelve inches, with the upper surface also coated with phosphorescent paint. The intention was for Spirit to move the trumpets, and use them for direct voice communication to whichever sitter the trumpet went.

With the plaque it was hoped to build up some form of physical manifestation. The first two meetings produced nothing noticeable. Then on the third, there was movement of both the trumpets and plaque. As time went on we began getting sounds through the trumpets, and unrecognisable forms building on the plaque. After about nine months, and since Christmas was approaching, messages were coming through the trumpets and there was a perfect Nativity scene, with miniature figures moving about on the plaque. Just as things were beginning to get interesting there was quite a lot in the press accusing some well-known physical mediums of fraudulence. This got me wondering and, after some thought, I decided to test it out, and see just how far one could go without being controlled. I said nothing to the sitters, but decided I would not be controlled, and see what I could do by myself. The seance got under way, I moved out of the cabinet, picked up the trumpets, and moved around the circle of sitters with comparative ease. This went on for some little while, then I returned to my seat, opened the curtains and announced the seance was finished. The sitters were naturally surprised at this outcome. I explained exactly what I had done, proving how easy it was to fake this form of phenomena, and I said I would not do it any more. So the circle closed with some regret, but I had satisfied myself that fraudulence was possible. I was not sorry to give it up, quite frankly, because for twenty-four hours after a seance it felt as though my whole inside had been pulled out, and it was very exhausting.

Three months went by, and then my controls said to me, 'You feel you have satisfied yourself over this form of mediumship. We would like you to repeat your last seance just one more time.' I said I would do this, and the necessary preparations having been made, we met again. We followed exactly the same pattern as before. I had hardly got out of the cabinet when I kicked someone's foot, and I found I could not put a foot anywhere without coming into contact with something or someone. I lost my sense of direction in the dark, and had some difficulty in getting back to my own chair. Having finally seated myself my control spoke to the sitters, thanking them for their cooperation, and saying, we just wanted to prove to you that Spirit control does not necessarily need deep trance conditions. On the previous occasion, although the medium was fully conscious of what he was doing, he was still under our control, and was thus able to move about the circle freely and easily. Tonight he was completely on his own, and the sitters saw the difference. This had been allowed to go on because it was no longer wished to continue this form of mediumship. Compared to the mediumship of John, mine was simple, but I suppose everything has to start somewhere. One thing the sitters missed when the circle closed was my little cockney boy Ginger. Another Ginger I thought, more trouble, I wonder?

He would always announce himself with a whistle and, "Ullo everyone, it's me, Ginger.' He told them, in reply to the question where did he live before he passed over, 'I didn't 'ave no 'ome, lived on the streets, never knew me Farver, and me Muvver died when I was five, so they put me in an 'ome, but I didn't like it so I run away.' When and how did he die? 'I was killed by a bomb in 'Ackney when I was nine.' He was as bright as a button, and used to keep them amused whilst the power was building up for the phenomena.

Among the members of the Temple were an Indian family, comprising father, mother and son. The father was quiet but with considerable wisdom; the son was in one of the study groups, and the mother we seldom saw. After some months the father asked Ruth and me if we would go and see his wife. She had asked to see us, and was a sick lady. We called, and she was indeed very sick. She had had cancer for quite a long time, and had not seen a doctor because she was too frightened. She should have been in hospital, but they all seemed completely helpless. They had not got a doctor, so we persuaded our own doctor to go and see her. This he did and was shocked at what he saw. He advised that she should go into hospital but she flatly refused. Alternatively the doctor recommended that a nurse should visit daily, but again this was refused – the husband protesting that he could manage. However, we could see they were very poor, so we paid for a night nurse to come in to assist. The nurse had been nursing cancer patients for several months and she just could not understand why the patient – who was the worst case she had ever seen – insisted she was in no pain, and this was indeed surprising seeing the state of her body. This created considerable interest in her towards healing, and we had some interesting discussions as a result.

The morning after the night the patient died, the nurse telephoned to tell us, and we went along, knowing that we would have to make all the necessary arrangements for the funeral. We went up into the bedroom and on going over towards the bed were brought to a sudden halt, just as though a glass screen had dropped down between us and the bed. We stood there somewhat nonplussed, then we saw what looked like a misty shape leaving the body of the patient, drifting upwards and away. Immediately, the unseen screen was removed, and we went to the bedside. For the first time we had witnessed the spirit leaving the physical body.

During the months of my physical mediumship training we sometimes experienced disturbances at night which would wake us up, not feeling too happy. I would send out a thought to White Eagle and, very soon, we would feel a stealthy movement, and a soft pressure across our legs, from which a quiet purring sound came. This was 'Tonga', the black panther, who was White Eagle's constant companion, and he would always come if there was any feeling of unrest, or disturbance. It was a very comforting feeling, every movement so beautifully smooth and graceful, bringing with it a feeling of complete security. Questioning White Eagle one day on this close relationship between the panther and himself, he told us this story.

He, White Eagle, had been the eldest son of a tribal chief and, as the first son would, in due course, become chief himself. From time to time, at night, a black panther had been seen carrying off babies from their encampment, but they had never been able to catch it. White Eagle was ordered to take a party of braves to catch and destroy the panther, and not return until this was done. Twenty of them set out, and he directed each one to cover certain areas, leaving very little space uncovered. On the seventh day, as the sun was going down, he came face to face with the creature. He drew his bow to take aim. How could he destroy this beautiful creature? They stood as though transfixed, neither making any move. He was a lover of life and beauty, and this creature was exquisite. He lowered his bow and, almost as though the animal read his mind, it came slowly forward to sit at his feet. This bond of complete trust each for the other, was almost uncanny and, from that moment, they were inseparable. He returned to the encampment with the panther at his side. Their arrival had not gone unnoticed, and his father appeared, demanding an explanation. He stated what had taken place, and his reluctance to kill the panther, to which his father replied: 'You have disobeyed my command, you have brought disgrace on me and our tribe. You are not fit to be my son, and you shall surely die with the wretched creature you have brought with you.' And so they died together, and have continued that close bond ever since.

We have often seen 'Tonga', and he really is a magnificent creature with beautiful rippling muscles, indication of great strength but, like White Eagle, who is big and powerful, they both have a wealth of love, compassion and understanding.

Some three weeks after the passing of our Indian lady friend, we had an urgent call late one night from a friend of Sally, our night nurse friend. Apparently Sally was ill and wanted us to go to Hampstead to see her. On arrival, I was standing at the foot of her bed and, on opening her eyes from a fitful sleep, she pointed at me, saying, 'That's exactly where I saw you when I asked Kathy to ring you. I feel dreadful.' We gave her healing, and she seemed to calm down, and go off to a more relaxed sleep. We left, telling her friend we would call next afternoon. When we arrived Kathy said she had to miss going to work as Sally had been delirious, and she could not leave her. We decided the best thing to do was take her back home with us, and nurse her back to health. She had been nursing terminally ill people for nine months without a break, and our patient had just tipped the scale, and she had broken down.

Sally was with us for a month and, when she was ready to leave, she told me she could not repay me with money, but that she would give me something which would be invaluable in my healing work. It was an old Maori method of stopping bleeding given to her by her father by an old Maori woman, to be passed from generation to generation, alternating male, female, male, female each time. I thanked her, and promptly forgot all about it from a practical point of view, except for laughingly talking about my magic way of stopping bleeding. Some long time later we had an urgent call from a friend – his wife had injured her hand badly while chopping wood and could I help? I was not available at the time, and the message was passed to me when I came out of the meeting. All I had to know was the person's names. I telephoned my friend as soon as I was free to say that I was commencing but fifteen minutes later he rang back to say that nothing had happened. He gave me his wife's names again, and it transpired that the person taking the message had got one of the christian names wrong. So I started again and five minutes later the telephone rang again. Apparently the bleeding had stopped almost as soon as I had put down the telephone. So the Maori method did work and it has proved a godsend many times since that first trial run.

☆ ☆ ☆

By 1956 we had been at the Temple for nine and a half years, wholly dedicated to it. It was our life but, strangely, now a kind of mild restlessness was beginning to show. Not with Fraser but with Ruth and myself. I could not put a finger on it, but the best way I could describe it was that I felt I could not breathe easily. I wanted to expand my lungs but the four walls would not let me. This feeling of restriction grew until circumstances provided the opportunity for us to leave what we had for so long felt was our whole life. We decided healing was our great love, so we bought a much larger house, and opened our own Sanctuary. The thought of possible failure never once entered our heads. It was a wonderful feeling of freedom, yet we owed it all to the excellent teaching of Mrs Rayner and Dr Lewis, who together had set our feet so firmly on the true spiritual pathway.

6

BRANCHING OUT

Remembering I still had my business to run and, with the return of fur fabrics on the market, the demand for our real skin toys was getting less and less. Orders from the wholesalers fell away, so I decided to go direct to the people they had been supplying. I saw the buyers at Harrods, Hamleys and other big stores, offering exactly what they had been buying but, at more competitive prices. The answers were all the same. They were quite satisfied with their present suppliers. It seemed, if one offered something cheaper it must be of inferior quality. Then a couple came along with big ideas of expansion. They had contacts in America and Canada. They would do the selling, and we the manufacture. They could see us soon opening factories in America and Canada, and who knew where else? They had several sample ranges, coming back from time to time for more. After six months they had given away about a hundred toys, without a single order. We discovered later they had been giving them away as presents to their friends.

So we finished with them, and then I had a call from the bank manager to say that we were heavily overdrawn and what were we going to do about it? We talked it over, and he agreed to take our stock of skins against the overdraft until we could sell them. Had we been able to buy fur fabrics I am sure the business would have flourished but, unless you were registered before the war for these fabrics, the manufacturers would not supply. We finally wound up the toy business with a sigh of relief.

I still had my auto-electrical concessionary business and we moved into the complete replacement of units, instead of repairing. With the development of this business, Ruth was, more and more, tied in the office, and needed me there rather than on the road. However, we knew of a young woman who had been sent to prison, but I visited her there and said she could have a job with me when she was released. I spoke to the authorities who released her into our care. She turned out to be the most hard working, honest and reliable person I have ever employed, and was a real asset to us.

The new house was quite a large one and, with just the two of us, we felt rather like 'peas in a drum' so decided to convert the upstairs to a self-contained flat, and let it to an Indian eye specialist.

Enjoying the freedom after ten years' involvement solely in the Temple gave us the opportunity of getting out among people, and seeing what was going on in the outside world. A free weekend was a unique experience, and we decided to buy a caravan, and site it on the River Blackwater at Stone in Essex, where we spent many very happy weekends. I bought an old fishing boat, and amused myself for hours making it seaworthy, so that I could enjoy my favourite pastime again on the water.

Some of my original patients from the Temple insisted on coming to me at home, and I started healing every Monday morning. Although the house was single fronted, it was deep with a large front room, long passage with two smaller rooms leading off, and another large back room. We used the front room for healing for a while, but local people got to know about the Sanctuary, and we had to extend the time to all day on Mondays.

Soon after we had started the Sanctuary I noticed a change in my method of working and was told by White Eagle that now we were an independent Centre, it was necessary to have a contol with medical knowledge and he, White Eagle, would be standing back, and Dr Paul Renault would be the principal healing control from now on. His presence was so different from that of White Eagle. I did not heal in trance, but was very aware of the healer's presence with me. Dr Paul Renault made me think of a robin – he was small of stature, very alert, and almost curt in his manner.

We did not want to work in isolation. We felt the need to expand, to meet others in the healing field, to exchange knowledge and experience, and we found just such an organisation. The National Federation of Spiritual Healers (NFSH) had been formed to unite healers from all parts of the country, where they could get together from time to time for 'talking shop' and working together. Its first member and president was the famous healer, Harry Edwards. I joined the NFSH in 1958 along with many well-known personalities, such as Gordon Turner, George and Olive Burton, Fred Doyle, Sid and Helen Staples and Percy and Laurie Wilson. I give an account of the NFSH's history in Chapter 7.

In 1959 we met Mary Martin who was vice-president of the newly formed Home Counties Association of Spiritual Healers, which was affiliated to the NFSH. We joined this association too and, before long I was its chairman. In this capacity I was its representative on the NFSH Council, getting to know many influential people in the field of healing. We struck up a friendship with Sid and Helen Staples. Sid was the NFSH Organising Secretary, and he persuaded me to become chairman of an NFSH sub-committee, which advised on Council matters.

We were certainly far from isolated now, and the Sanctuary was growing apace too. So much so, that in 1960, we completely reorganised the whole of the ground floor. We moved upstairs into the flat and knocked the wall down between the front room and the one behind it, curtaining off the opening with blue shot velvet curtains. The front room became the waiting room and the inner room the main healing room. The next one had been a kitchen. It was now Ruth's animal healing room. Next down the passage were toilet facilities, and the back room was partitioned off into four healing cubicles.

Soon after we started, there was much interest in our work, and I was asked if I would start a developing group. We had two groups of seven for healing development almost from the start. Patients treated had now reached a remarkable 160 per week, and these trainees had been getting plenty of practice, under supervision. Now, some of them could work on their own.

We have always considered a pleasant atmosphere to be important, and tried to provide this whenever possible. The waiting room was large, airy and carpeted, with pastel walls, and curtains to blend. There were flowers, soft background music and, very important, a caring, sympathetic and understanding receptionist. Every trainee healer had to serve a period as receptionist. One patient's specialist paid us a visit, curious to see the place which had helped his patient so much and he was very impressed with the Sanctuary's happy atmosphere.

One of the receptionists had a grandson, and he came to the Sanctuary with his mother. He had to have surgery next day to remove his tonsils, which were diseased. He came into the healing room, sat on his mother's knee and told me how sore his throat was. He couldn't eat very well!! He was four years old and quite a bright little chap. They went to the hospital next day, they looked at his throat, and sent them home again. There was nothing wrong, everything was quite normal and healthy! They came back next week to tell me all about it. When his turn came, the little chap came in by himself, he didn't need his mother. He could tell me himself. He climbed up on the stool saying he wanted some more healing, he liked it! I remember this was November because, a few weeks later, he was Christmas shopping with his parents, and he wanted to get a present for Uncle Gilbert. They went from shop to shop but he could not find anything until, in desperation, his father said they must go home, had no more time. Halfway home Wing called out, 'Stop, Daddy, stop, I've seen what I want.' There was nothing in sight but a stonemason's yard.

'What is it you want then, there's nothing here.'

'Yes, I want that,' pointing to a large stone cross.

'Whatever for?'

'I want to put it in Uncle Gilbert's front garden so that everyone will know he works for Jesus!'

Early in the next year I had my first cancer patients – three breast cancers in three consecutive weeks. They had come, prior to surgery, for any help we might be able to give. With the first one the whole breast was hard, and a mastectomy was planned later that week. After a few minutes' healing the breast was nice and soft, with no obvious lumps. The patient telephoned me later in the week to say the consultant was delighted – examination had found no indication of anything wrong. The next week a similar case came in, except that here there was a large, hard lump. After healing, this had changed into a soft pocket. On reporting at hospital, this patient was examined, fluid drawn off from this 'pocket' and told the breast was now all right.

The third case was Ruth. She had a lump the size of a hen's egg in the left breast, and had persuaded the doctor to give her a week to see if healing would do anything. During the healing I found my fingers kneading the lump and, looking at her face, was surprised to see how composed she was, with no sign of discomfort (this had been painful to the touch) and I felt it disappearing under my fingers. This too vanished without trace, not to return.

Another interesting incident was that of a 'breach' birth. This was causing some concern, and the woman came to us as a last hope. I rested my hands lightly on her abdomen, and felt the baby move right round into its correct position for birth. No pressure or manipulation, just this unseen intelligence and power working under natural law to give an easy, natural birth. Another woman came to us with duodenal ulcers. She was very sceptical but was amazed that after a few minutes on the healing stool the ulcer disappeared.

We used to discuss any interesting case at the end of the day, and this one certainly came under discussion. Why, we thought, should someone like that receive spontaneous healing when others, much more spiritual, sometimes did not. This woman did not come again, but we learned from the person who brought her, that although she continued to eat foods that were bad for duodenal ulcers, she still remained free of pain, and the ulcers did not return. We also heard later that her character had subsequently changed too, from her former self-centred attitude, and was now going out of her way to help people. Thus it is interesting to see how healing on one level will affect another. In this case the healing on the physical level had also affected the emotional and spiritual levels of consciousness.

When we extended our healing clinic, taking over the whole ground floor, it was officially opened, and dedicated, by Mary Martin – vice-president of the Home Counties Association of Spiritual Healers, and herself an excellent healer and medium. The waiting room was large enough to seat fifty people, and we had lectures and demonstrations on a regular basis, with the result that 4 Meadowcroft Road, Palmers

Green, became a healing and teaching centre with quite a large following.

The lectures and demonstrations were held on weekends, and one Saturday evening I had just come out of trance after giving a talk when the telephone rang. It was a very distraught young woman who explained that she was a Catholic, had been very ill and gone to a healer for help, and had been healed. She had been so happy and grateful that she went to see her priest to tell him and give thanks, but he ordered her out of the church and said she had consorted with the Devil, and would be damned for the rest of her life. She was now too scared to go home to her parents. I explained that the priest, in his ignorance, was closer to the Devil than she. He was supposed to be a spiritual leader, and he was bringing shame on his church, not her. I told her to go home and tell her parents what had happened – I knew they would understand and that she had nothing to fear. We would pray for her, and thank God for her recovery. We would also pray that light be brought into the darkened mind of her priest. We heard no more from her but our spirit friends told us that her parents had strongly condemned the priest, and had left his church.

Among the many visiting mediums and healers lecturing was one we got very attached to – Nan MacKenzie. She was a real workaholic for Spirit. On her first visit at Meadowcroft Road she gave a talk followed by some clairvoyance. I was chairing the meeting and, just before we closed, she turned to me and told me that I would soon grow out of the Sanctuary. I protested, but she was adamant.

It was not long after this that we got shock news about our business premises. The garage owner had sold out, and the new owner was going to knock down the lockups, and extend the garage. So we had to look for new premises. After exhaustive searching all we could find was a large double-fronted shop in Winchmore Hill, two miles away. We did not want the shop, but it had ideal storage space at the back with a driveway for vehicles. We had no option but to take it, and I decided we would open the shop as a boat chandlers – an echo of my old love of sailing. Again, it was poor Ruth who would have to stay behind and manage things when I had to be out on the road.

After a hectic two weeks of racking the stores and fitting out the shop 'Andy's Boathouse' came into being. For the first few months it seemed that whatever the customer wanted we did not have it in spite of having three hundred different items. However, we usually managed to obtain the items within a week, and this was appreciated, and so business started to build up. We had plenty of room in the shop, so we had some speedboats on display, together with a couple of sailing dinghies and outboard motors. We soon had customers from the Welsh Harp at Hendon, and various sailing clubs on the river Lea. However, we had some unfortunate experiences with some of our 'customers'. We often discovered that items had been stolen, for example a compass removed from its box. Also, our first speedboat sale was to the value of £1,900, but this was bought on hire purchase. Unfortunately the 'purchaser' defaulted on his payments, and apart from his initial ten per cent deposit, we were unable to reclaim neither the money nor the boat.

We had taken on the London agency for a Norfolk firm of boat kit manufacturers and their sales manager came down to assist me on one occasion with one of my boat-building demonstrations. When he arrived he was doubled up with pain from an ulcer. I took him into the back of the shop, and gave him healing for it, and he seemed much better, so we got on with the demonstration. He went off next morning saying how much better he felt. Business with their kits was going very well, and they offered us an extended area of representation, and to be on their stand at the Earls Court Boat Show. We went up to their works for a weekend to finalise arrangements and, in conversation, they said how thrilled Brian (the sales manager) was at his healing. They enquired whether healing worked for animals because they had rescued a steeple chaser from being put down because it had developed arthritis in its forelegs. We went into the paddock where there was a lovely grey horse hobbling about. The joints were swollen and inflamed, so we spent about five minutes on the joints, and running down both legs, hoping it would do some good. Six months later we had a telephone call to say that Silver had made a dramatic recovery after our visit and had since been winning rosettes in local gymkhanas.

Some little while later, I had been up to their Norfolk works again, and brought back a twenty-six foot four-berth cruiser, which I put on display in front of the shop, and it certainly caused considerable interest. One day I was outside talking to a would-be customer, and saw a gipsy type of person go into the shop, but thought no more about it. Later in the day Ruth said she had had a visit from a gipsy, trying to sell her lace, and who also insisted on telling her fortune, which was that we would be out of that place within twelve months. We laughed and promptly forgot the incident.

An old friend, the one who started the pre-war flying club, told me of a nice site at Waterbeach, near Cambridge, with a pleasant river frontage. It belonged to the pub called The Bridge and we rented this delightful plot from the owner. We had our own private mooring, and just below us the Cambridge Motor Boat Club – rather 'County' don't you know – and below them the sailing club, which I joined. Before leaving Stone I had sold the fishing boat hull, and bought a sailing dinghy, which was more suitable for inland river sailing.

This friend of ours lived at Hatfield, and we used to go over from time to time, because he was building himself a cabin cruiser. When it was nearing completion he ran into financial business problems, and decided he'd have to sell *Kitty 1*, as he'd christened it. Kitty was his wife's name, but she wasn't included in the sale! I offered to buy it, and the great day arrived for its transportation to Waterbeach. It was very well-built, and heavy, so had to go on a low loader. We had the true launching ceremony with champagne, and she was afloat. Jim, Kitty and Chris, their son, Ruth and myself, with a small knot of onlookers wondering if it was going to sink! Jim asked if they could have it for a week's holiday as from then? Seeing he'd spent nearly a year building it, I could hardly refuse. We returned home and left them to enjoy its first week of freedom on the River Cam. We arrived next weekend to find considerable commotion. I would mention here that, not only were the members of the Motor Boat Club weekend sailors, but only about three of the twenty craft there had left their moorings in years. They just lay there year in, year out, owners polishing everything they could lay their hands on that would outshine their neighbour. But tragedy had struck. The largest of the fleet had been hit amidships, and there was a large dent in the hull. Enquiring what had happened, Jim, in his infinite wisdom, had let nine-year-old Chris take the controls and, deciding to turn the boat round, chose to do it opposite the moored craft, found he could not do it in one sweep, forgot to put it into reverse, and picked the biggest one to hit right in the middle. We never did make friends at the Motor Boat Club!! *Kitty 1,* built like a tank, was not even marked.

7

INVOLVEMENT WITH THE NFSH

I will start this chapter by giving a short history of the National Federation of Spiritual Healers. In November 1948, John Britnell BEM gave his first demonstration of spiritual healing in a small church at Forest Gate, London. Within a year he had gathered around him a small band of healers and formed the Essex Healers' Association. From this humble beginning an organisation was built up to having a membership of some hundreds of accredited healers and associate members.

It was found then that healers were seeking membership from all over the United Kingdom and the result was the foundation of the National Federation of Spiritual Healers in June 1954. The founding members were John Britnell, William Prince, Gordon Turner and Fred Doyle. Support was received from Harry Edwards who became member number one. Percy and Laurie Wilson drew up the first constitution in which it was resolved that the NFSH should be non-denominational.

At the first Annual General Meeting held in the Ilford church in 1955 four county associations were represented having a membership of seven hundred healers and associates. Since then the progress of the NFSH had been remarkable. Within ten years the membership exceeded two thousand accredited healers, over two thousand associate members and, in a new form of membership created in 1962, some hundreds of probationary members who are training to become fully qualified healers.

In recent years the influence of the NFSH has become worldwide, and hundreds of healers in other lands have enrolled as members. Following this, healers' associations have been formed in Canada, Australia, New Zealand and South Africa. Liaison officers are establishing territorial associations in the United States. There are NFSH representatives in European countries too. All of these give allegiance to the NFSH.

In 1960 the Hospital Authorities and Management Committees in Great Britain were asked if they would give permission for members of the NFSH to visit the sick (with medical sanction) in the hospitals under their jurisdiction – 268 authorities gave this permission, thus entitling our members to have entry in over 1,600 hospitals. When the British Medical Council became aware of this, it asked the hospital authorities to cancel their permissions and sponsored questions in the House of Commons seeking the Minister of Health's veto, but the Minister refused to give this. As a result of the BMA campaign only twenty-three authorities withdrew their sanctions, so that in 1964 our members retained the privilege to attend the sick in over 1,500 national hospitals.

The passing of its Founder Chairman, John Britnell, in December 1957, was a sad blow to the NFSH. He was a man of pleasing personality, sincerity, vision and drive as well as possessing a fine healing gift. We treasure his memory today. It was largely as a result of his early years of pioneering work that the NFSH has built up the high prestige it now enjoys with its recognition by the national press and its acceptance as a charitable institution.

Summer schools were started in 1964, under the directorship of the late Gordon Turner and have been held annually since. The first school was held in London; the second in the Keble and Oriel Colleges in Oxford, and then later at Mallon Dene in Sussex. This is the only school of its kind in the world and representatives from many countries arrive each year to join the three hundred and more students from the United Kingdom.

The Federation has issued a number of pamphlets to all its members to encourage the nobility and understanding of healing practice. These include the report of a special committee that devoted two years to the study of healership in all its aspects. Special advice and leaflets are circulated on legal and other matters associated with healing practice. Every full member in the United Kingdom is insured against loss through negligence to the amount of £50,000.

Healers' Day celebrations have been held annually in the Royal Festival Hall, London (at the Fairfields Hall, Croydon 1963/64) to capacity audiences, which have been followed by mass healing services in the evenings. It is now the general practice to follow up all propaganda services organised by the NFSH by mass healing services. By this means many thousands of sick people have had an opportunity of receiving healing treatment throughout the land.

History was made on Whit Sunday 1964 when the first open-air demonstration of spiritual healing was given in Trafalgar Square, London, by Harry Edwards and George Burton. This was organised by the Surrey Healers' Association and received wide publicity in the national press and the cinema. A healing documentary film was prepared based on this occasion.

In 1953, an Archbishop's Commission was appointed to find the means of restoring spiritual healing into the pastoral work of the church. The President, Harry Edwards, was invited to speak to the Commission and provide factual evidence of super-normal spiritual healings. In May 1956 the British Medical Association published its report on behalf of the Commission and made this statement: 'We can find no evidence that there is any type of illness cured by spiritual healing alone which could not have been cured by medical treatment.' Another statement read: 'Recoveries take place through spiritual healing which cannot be accounted for by medical science.' It will be observed in both statements that the BMA admits that spiritual healing is a reality.

In the same report a warning was issued to doctors against cooperating with healers under penalty of disciplinary action. In spite of this an ever-increasing number of physicians are supporting spiritual healing (in confidence) and advising their patients to seek it.

When the Commission's report was published, its negative attitude and refusal to consider the evidence that was submitted to it induced the NFSH in cooperation with the Spiritualist Association of Great Britain to conduct a protest meeting in the Royal Albert Hall, London. Before a capacity audience the living testimony of some of the cases submitted to the Commission was presented to the public.

In addition to the general work of the NFSH as so far mentioned, it should be remembered that the main work of its members continues daily in the many churches, sanctuaries and homes of healers at home and abroad, voluntarily and without fees. Those who cannot visit the places of healing are visited in their homes by its members. The progress and prestige of the NFSH has been built up upon success in healing the sick often when medical science can do no more.

As already mentioned, the NFSH summer schools have been one of its great successes. There have been a few changes to the original formula, including the change of venue in 1967 to the Overmead Hotel in Torquay, and in 1969 I took over the directorship.

Another regular and important function of the NFSH was the organising of public healing demonstrations all over the country, and this was the job of Syd Staples, the organising secretary. He was an excellent organiser, and did a marvellous job with anything to do with large meetings of any kind. There were meetings with several thousand people, and this was almost a monthly occurrence with visits to places such as Leeds, Watford, Plymouth, Hastings, Oxford, Bournemouth, Torquay, Guildford and, of course, London. Added to these many functions were 'healers day' every year, the annual dinner dance in London, and the annual re-dedication service held each year at the Harry Edwards Sanctuary at Shere. This event was always part of the summer school programme, and we would go from the school to Burrows Lea for this very popular service.

We also had the pleasure of opening a Healing Sanctuary in South Wales in 1960 which has now developed into a magnificent church under the leadership of its founder, Marian Butler.

As chairman of Home Counties Association of Spiritual Healers I got to know a number of groups and churches, one of which was a small church at Potters Bar. They had worked hard for a long time, and just acquired new premises, and I was invited to dedicate its opening. It was here, after the service, we met a lady who asked if we could help her Pekinese dog. It was blind in one eye. This lady turned out to be a matron at a local hospital, with whom we built up a very strong friendship. She was very interested in our healing work and the Sanctuary, and soon joined the developing group. Through her, we became friendly with the senior orthopaedic surgeon at the hospital, and inevitably healing would come into the conversation. I explained that spiritual healing was not a physical energy, but a divine one that was manifest **THROUGH** us not **OF** us. We often talked about it, and some of the remarkable healings that had taken place, particularly that of a young girl who we had treated at the Sanctuary. For several years her bones had been crumbling, and walking was both painful and difficult. She was one of his patients, and he was amazed that after six months' healing, the bone structure had re-built, and everything was fine again.

One morning he telephoned me asking for help. He had to undertake a difficult operation at ten o'clock that morning and wanted me to 'link up' with him at that time, as he felt sure it would help. Later that evening he rang to thank me, saying it was, as he anticipated, a very difficult case. Nothing had seemed to be going right, but then after stopping for a few moments and 'linking up', it was as though he was being inspired, everything going so smoothly once again. He could see his old professor in his mind. After this, he would always ask for help when difficulties seemed imminent, and it never failed.

Resulting from this, one of the hospital doctors asked our matron friend, Billy, if she thought I could help a student nurse who was gravely ill with peritonitis, and had slipped into a coma. Billy and I went to see her and found her lying in a cot absolutely rigid, as though carved out of wood. I stood with my hands about twelve inches above her body for possibly five minutes then, with a slight sigh, all the tension went out of her body, and she completely relaxed. Opening her eyes, she smiled at Matron, turned on her side, and went into a perfectly relaxed sleep.

After this dramatic turn-round the doctors decided to go back to the drug treatment she had been on previously. I protested saying I would prefer nature to restore her health, but this was ignored. After two days she started a fever again. I protested once more, and still it was ignored. Dr Paul, my spirit control, told me not to worry, they would attend to it.

Next day, each time she took the drug, her temperature went up higher and higher, until it was imperative the treatment was stopped. As soon as it stopped, the temperature returned to normal, and she made steady progress. After three months' convalescence she returned to resume her nursing.

When Billy took over as Matron, there were about fifty encephalitic patients who had been there since the First World War. This condition is a degenerative disease of the brain, which will ultimately leave the individual like a 'cabbage'. They were dressed in the old workhouse type of blue dress, with literally nothing in their life at all. One had been a professional ballet dancer, another an artist, another a singer, and they had been reduced to this for the last forty years. Billy decided that they should be treated like human beings and arranged for them to get new clothes. This produced a transformation – it was like a rebirth for some of them, and an interest in what was going on began to show. Billy really transformed the patients' hitherto empty lives, and they really loved her for what she had done for them.

One Christmas we had a party in her house with Tom and Mary Patterson; Tom was secretary of the International Spiritual Federation with contacts in many countries, Ella Sheridan of the Greater World Christian Spiritualist Headquarters in London, June, a friend of ours and a group member, Billy, Ruth and myself.

Tom wanted to make contact with spirit, and asked me to go into trance. I did so, and Dr Paul came through answering questions put to him, then White Eagle spoke about their work in the other world, and introduced a personality best known to Mr Patterson. This personality came through, and introduced himself as Conan Doyle, and talked at length to Tom about his connections overseas. When told of this after the seance, I found it hard to believe. I'd never had anyone like that through before, but Tom had no doubts as to his authenticity. Speech, voice, mannerisms and knowledge of Tom's work were undeniably correct. He also told us of the impending visit of some influential people from Japan that none of us had any knowledge of but, sure enough, within a week Tom had a letter advising their coming. He brought them over to our Sanctuary which pleased them very much, and they spent two days with us. Their object was a world tour investigating spiritual healing in different countries, and their ultimate findings were that, no matter what religious beliefs different countries had, basically it was all the same, but dressed up a little differently. We took them out to lunch, and it was interesting to see the reaction of our local people. The men wore European dress, but the ladies dressed in their national costume which was most colourful and attractive. The thing that interested most people, I think, was the tiny feet of the two ladies! It is said that the Japanese face is expressionless but, when the time came for them to leave us, the ladies had tears in their eyes, they had so enjoyed their visit. The interpreter told us they had come to England with some trepidation, not knowing what sort of welcome they would receive after the war, but we found them very ordinary likeable people, and enjoyed their company.

Back in the Sanctuary, after we had been there for about two years, a reporter from *Psychic News*, Philip Paul, called in to interview us. Seeing how busy it was, he asked whether we charged fees or accepted donations – the answer was no to both of these. He then pointed out that we could be depriving some people of the opportunity of showing their appreciation for the help we gave them. He suggested we have a plate that patients could put a donation in if they wanted to. And if we didn't want the money we could give it to others who did need it. We had not thought of it in that way before, but it made sense. We began to see the wisdom of his remarks – six nights of the week the place was ablaze with light, with healing sessions or groups going on, and, throughout the winter months the heating and lighting bills grew enormously. We began to need replacement carpets and chairs too – so here we were, faced with some heavy outgoings that we had not considered in our enthusiasm to heal the sick.

By now we were very busy at the Sanctuary and Ruth worked there most days – I had taken on a man to do my auto-electrical rounds, and the girl we had given a job to was coping well in the office and shop. George and Olive Bell had sessions two days a week, Phillip and Vivienne Woodcock two evenings, Fred and Jean Feast two evenings and Sid and Helen Staples also had a Monday clinic.

However, not everybody was happy to donate to the work of the Sanctuary. We helped the wife of a very wealthy man to recover from a nervous breakdown. She had been housebound for four years and was covered with psoriasis. After a visit from me, she was persuaded to visit the Sanctuary, which she did for six months. After that, she went away with her husband and he forbade her from contacting us again – and he had been very reluctant to make any kind of donation to our work.

Dr Fisher, a GP living close to our Sanctuary, had occasion to go into hospital for surgery and, knowing that Billy, our matron friend, was connected with us, asked her if I would go and give him healing. I arrived at his bedside when his daughter was there. He told her to sit down while I gave him healing, then I left them together again. Billy overheard their conversation after I left. 'Father, why on earth did you, a Jew, allow that man, a Gentile, to heal you?' His answer was, 'My dear, if you and I were going to St Paul's in London, I went by train, and you decided to go by bus, we would both arrive at the same destination. Does that answer your question?'

Out of the blue one day we had a call from an aunt of mine – a neighbour of hers had a very mentally handicapped baby. She was, in fact, two years old, and the verdict of the hospital was that she was just a piece of living flesh, with no reactions at all. The hospital's advice to the distraught mother was to put her away in a home and forget her. However, the family had seen a television programme about Harry Edwards and had taken the child to him once, but it was a difficult journey for ordinary country folk without a car – they lived in Gamlingay, Bedfordshire, and Harry Edwards was at Shere in Surrey. He had said he thought there might be some hope for the child if she could have regular healing, and so the mother had been talking about this to my aunt who said, 'I've got a nephew who does healing, would you like me to speak to him about it?' We agreed to visit at the weekend, and met this pathetic little mite, Unice. She could not sit up, but just crumpled into a heap – her whole spine was like rubber. Her eyes were rolled up into the head and, if she fell over from being in a sitting position, there was no reaction whatever in facial expression or muscle response. She was, to all intents, as the hospital had said, just living flesh.

We healed Unice, and spent some time with the mother who needed help just as much as Unice. The child needed her constant attention, and there were two other young daughters, and a husband, to look after. So her life was very stressful and full. We agreed to visit again in a month's time and this second visit was much the same as the first, with no visible change. On the third visit, the mother held her in a sitting position on her lap. After a few minutes I told the mother to loosen her hold a bit on Unice for a moment and, to our joy, she remained upright for several seconds before the spine sagged. So there was the beginning of a response. The fourth visit we looked forward to with hopeful anticipation of continuing progress. Now Unice could sit for several minutes, provided she could be kept upright but, if she toppled over, there was still no visible sign of response of either nerve, or muscle.

Our fifth visit we will never forget. We were just finishing healing her – she had been sitting, without being held, for several minutes, except for our hands as we healed her and, as we took our hands away, she swayed to the left as though about to fall, and an expression of surprise appeared on her face. Then her eyes rolled down revealing two of the most beautiful blue eyes I had ever seen. We thought we had seen so-called miracles before, but this was really breathtaking.

Just before our seventh visit my aunt rang to say the strain of nearly three years' struggle had caught up with the mother, and Unice was being put into a mental home for children at St Neots, and asked if we would visit her there instead. We contacted the matron of the mental home beforehand and she agreed to our going. We arrived early one Sunday afternoon, met Matron, and told her briefly what we did, suggesting she should be with us while we healed Unice. She agreed and, after we had finished, she showed us over the home. There were thirty children there aged between a few weeks' old up to nine years – after the age of nine they were transferred to another home in Norwich.

To anyone new to this form of disability, it would have been heartbreaking. They were more like little animals than human beings. One little lad had had epileptic fits, and had to wear a crash helmet all the time, because he spent his days banging his head on the walls and floor. Another boy skated about on his bottom at considerable speed. On seeing us, he came over, climbed up me like a monkey, with one arm round my neck, and the other hand dipping into my pocket saying, 'Choc-choc' – he had obviously been used to searching out sweets in this way. En route, we met the senior nursing sister, who introduced us to a little girl, who sat facing into a corner all day long, clutching a plastic rattle. We stood watching her as the sister told us of this odd behaviour, then the child looked round and handed me her rattle. The matron and sister were amazed at this because the little girl would give neither of them her rattle. All in all, they were a pathetic but loveable collection, and so responsive to love and affection. Before we departed the matron invited us into her room for tea, and she said how pleased she was at the reaction of the children to us and asked us to visit again.

A journalist heard about our going there, and asked if he could come with us next time. Matron said all right, provided he didn't disrupt the normal routine. We did the rounds treating most of the children. One lady stopped to thank us for helping her son. She lived up in Yorkshire, and couldn't get down very often, and said she would be so grateful if we would see him whenever we came here. Rounds completed, we went into matron's room for tea. We had quite forgotten our journalist until he spoke up. 'I just do not understand it. I followed you round, did exactly as you did, but I got no response from the kids, why? I have got children of my own, I love kids, but I just could not get through.' I said, 'Well, it is easy really. It is not US that they respond to, it is the spiritual love that is put through us – the God-force that they recognise and respond to. It is an all-embracing love.'

Our visits there continued for two years, during which time Unice had learned to dress and feed herself, was learning to talk and respond to her own family. Then, in its infinite wisdom, the government decided it was too costly to keep the home open, closed it, and scattered the children all over the place to different homes or hospitals. We like to think that our visits there gave some of those youngsters a slightly better chance in life than they might have had without them.

Since we had started our own Sanctuary, we had encountered so many different forms of illness, disease or disability, it seemed there could not be many healthy people in the district. One problem that was very prevalent was back trouble. We helped many people with agonising slipped discs.

I may have just been fortunate with these cases, but they would respond in just a few minutes without any form of physical manipulation. Medically they would be put in a steel, or plaster corset for months, only to find that the vertebrae had fused together restricting movement. I found all I needed to do was to run my hand lightly down the spine to the affected area, hold it there for maybe a minute or two, then when I felt movement under my hand, would ask the patient to bend slowly forward. Nine times out of ten they would say that would not be possible but I would tell them to try and stop when it began to hurt. They would bend forward until they could touch their toes. The act of bending forward stretched the spine and, as they did so, I felt the disc slip back into its normal position. They could then straighten up, and wriggle about to their heart's content, without any vestige of discomfort.

We explained this, and even demonstrated it to doctors, but still the doctors stoically refused to accept its reality, making the excuse that they had either wrongly diagnosed slipped discs in the first place, or it was one of those strange cases where there would have been an improvement anyway whether we had been there, or not. It was impossible to win with many of them. If things did not happen according to their book of rules, it could not work. They seemed to elevate themselves above God, and knew all the possible answers to everything, quite forgetting that they were dealing with physical problems which were more often than not the final indication of some trouble originating from one of the more subtle areas of our being such as the emotions, mind, soul or spirit.

Spiritual healing is directed and governed by highly intelligent beings (ministering angels) whose knowledge is far superior to our material understanding. We, as healing instruments, do not claim any particular powers – we are very ordinary people who have been inspired to give time and study to the more spiritual levels of life, and have been privileged to be used by these higher spiritual beings to help alleviate suffering among very materially minded people. We readily acknowledge the value of medicine and scientific progress, at the same time regretting that the drug industry has taken over medicine. Because of this, they should acknowledge the existence of additional methods of help which, in most cases, do not have any harmful side effects. On one of our question evenings Dr Paul was asked whether the months I had been trained for physical mediumship had been a waste of time. His answer was, 'No, nothing is wasted, all experiences have a value.' In the case of my medium the training was necessary in instances where an energy was required with misplacements, or the movement of any physical matter. That was one of the reasons we were successful with most spinal problems, which required a form of psychic manipulation.

Ruth Anderson – serious illnesses overcome by healing after medical help failed.

Ruth and Gilbert welcoming guests at the Home Counties Association of Spiritual Healers Annual Dinner.

Laying on of hands following a demonstration in London by the late Harry Edwards.

Left to right:
Gilbert and Ruth Anderson, Harry Edwards, Olive and George Burton.

National Federation of Spiritual Healing Summer School at Overmead Hotel, Torquay, 1970.

Friday night is party night at the end of Summer School. Seen here Gilbert with his Troupe of Male Fairies.

The Denton Sanctuary.

Outlook from Sanctuary and waiting room.

New signs of life from our first pilot groups of cancer patients.

Cancer group in Nature Cure Clinic, London, showing the Biofeedback Instrument.

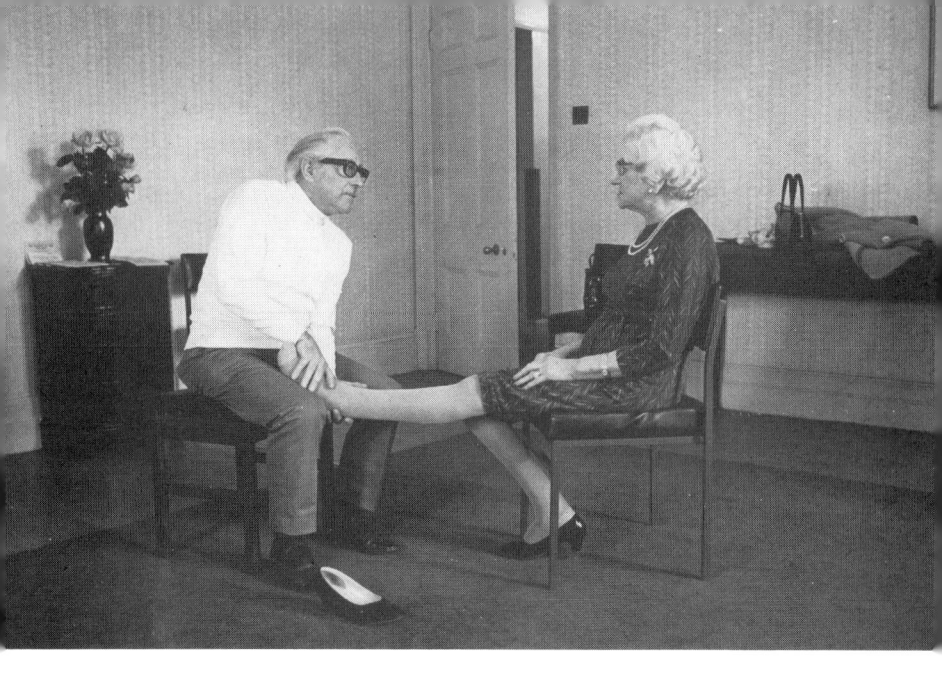

Gilbert healing a patient prior to her hundredth birthday.

World Federation of Healing stand, at Festival of Mind, Body and Spirit, London.

8

WE MOVE TO NORFOLK AGAIN – THEN BACK TO LONDON

Back to the realities of the business world, and boating in particular, we had been supplying a young man, who had built a thirty-foot sloop, with all the equipment for fitting it out. He had told us his intention was to live on board, and see how much of the world he could visit. He invited us to attend the launch along with the local press and television. A few days before the launch he came into the shop for a few more oddments, and gave Ruth a cheque for £1,550 to clear his account. However, a few days later, on arrival at the launching site we found the place deserted. We made enquiries at the boatyard, and found that our client and his boat had left ten days earlier. Next morning I rang the firm he worked for, only to be told he left them two weeks ago. I then telephoned his bank, and was told he had closed the account the previous week. His cheque was not met, and again he and his money (or our money) had gone. Extensive enquiries were made but as we had no real description of the boat, nothing ever came of it.

We had relied on this money to clear our own accounts, and thus the outlook was getting rather bleak. We ran the business down simply because we could not afford to restock, and finally we had a meeting with our auditor and solicitor. The auditor advised closing down the business because debts were piling up. Our 'sideline' had developed into a serious headache. The solicitor's advice was a bit of a surprise to me. He suggested we go bankrupt, because that way we would not have to pay off our debts. I felt extremely uncomfortable at the thought of making other people pay for my mistakes – I decided that I would rather sell my home to clear my debts. I could not live with the thought of passing my troubles on to other people. The solicitor thought I was mad, and left me to brood on the situation. When I got home Ruth said he had already spoken to her, telling her what he had advised, but she agreed with my decision to clear our debts no matter what. So we sold off stock as cheaply as we could, and what was left we offered back to the suppliers for what they would give us. Finally, we sold the house and our home, being left with £100 after all the debts had been cleared.

We found a temporary furnished flat situated on the North Circular Road at a junction. Outside the flat was a cigarette machine, and it seemed as though every other lorry that came along stopped there for cigarettes, with screeching brakes, then moved off only to stop again a few yards further on for traffic lights. This went on non-stop right through the night. After a few nights we thought we would go mad. Pondering one night what we should do, we decided that we would have a clinic at the flat, and the other healers from the Sanctuary would work from their own homes, and in this way they could establish their own centres, and start training others. We asked Dr Paul what we should do, it was obvious this present flat was not suitable, and his advice was to start looking further afield for a new home.

We spent several weekends scouring Hertfordshire, only to find prices ridiculously high. After all, you cannot buy a lot with £100. After three depressing weekends we were told to extend our area of search. Our boat kit suppliers in Norfolk offered us the use of a cottage annexe they had attached to their house. It was there for friends, if they were prepared to look after themselves. We could use it as long as we liked, and use it as a base from which to look around. This was the end of May, and our friends 'upstairs' had told us we would find what we were looking for in June. We got property details from every conceivable source, and started each weekend with a stack of leaflets describing desirable properties, most of which were really not fit to keep pigs in, let alone human beings. So our search continued until we reached the last day of June. We had seen seven properties, and were disgusted with them all. It was nearly three o'clock in the afternoon and we were hungry and fed up. I said, 'There must always be a first time, our friends have let us down this time, let's pack up and go home.' We returned to the cottage, packed up, and made for home. Two miles out I stopped at a signpost marked 'Denton 1½ miles'. This rang a bell because I was sure we had some details about a property in Denton. We went through our pile of papers, and there at the foot of another property was just two lines describing a bungalow. Since we were so near, we decided to have a look at it. We went up a winding lane, then it came into view. Almost before we saw it I said, 'That's it.' It was ideal – a nice bungalow with plenty of ground, and a large prefabricated shell as a garage which would be an ideal store for my electrical goods. We knocked on the door and were told that the owners already had a prospective buyer – however, this would-be purchaser had another property to sell, and we were unencumbered by that problem. The owners decided they would prefer to sell to us because they were anxious to move, but they wanted a ten per cent deposit – which was £300 – straight away. However, I contacted a friend who was willing to lend me the money and so the purchase went through. We moved in on 1 August wondering if we had gone completely mad. We had left a very busy centre in London and, here we were, out in a country village without public transport. The nearest bus service was one and a half miles away, with only two buses a day, one to Norwich and one to Lowestoft. What kind of healing service could we present there?

After the removal van had left we stood surveying the scene, and our acquisition. The previous owner had been a market gardener, and we had two and a half acres of land on which he had grown crops, which we now wanted as grass. The bungalow was fine. The prefabricated shed was large enough to house a 'transit' van, and three cars, plus the several tons of electrical gear waiting for racking round the walls. With plenty to look forward to workwise, we thought it might be good to have a year or so to get sorted out before we thought about healing. However, the next afternoon the telephone rang – it was a lady who had been on Harry Edwards's healing list but now wanted some contact healing and Harry Edwards had told her about our moving to this area. So within less than twenty-four hours we already had our first patient. And from that first patient numbers grew and by the end of September we had twenty coming.

Our twelve months' respite was a non-starter and, by June the following year, we had added a sixty feet by ten feet extension to the back of the bungalow, as a healing Sanctuary. This was opened officially by Harry Edwards and our local rector, Bob Close. It was a grand day, with sixty people from all parts of the country attending.

During the ten months we had been there we had levelled the ground and grass seeded it. I dug out a pond backed with a rockery and waterfall. We had fish and water lilies in it, together with a fountain. The waiting room looked out on to this, and patients were quite happy if they had to wait in this very pleasant atmosphere. The local people were marvellous. The local women took over the task of providing, and serving, refreshments, refusing to take payment for the super things they provided, and some of the men had given a hand on levelling the ground. Our friend Billy loved it, and was with us practically every weekend, and we had agreed that we would build on to the bungalow for her retirement. Also, with the help of a foreman bricklayer who lived in the village, we extended the frontage of the bungalow by another twenty-five feet and the overall depth by ten feet, so that we had added almost another third to its original size.

After three years the lawns had developed beautifully, and we held garden parties and morris dancing on the back lawns. In front of the garage/store we had a very attractive shrub lawn while in front of the bungalow a plain lawn again. I was all for ease of working, and cutting grass seemed to be the easiest way of keeping a large garden although, doing this amount with an ordinary lawn mower, was both exhausting and time consuming. However, I managed to obtain a 'ride-on' mower by exchanging a plough and rotovator (which the previous owner had left behind) for one and this made a tremendous difference to my labour. What used to take me two whole days I could now get through in half a day.

You may be wondering how I managed to buy the bungalow. Having got the loan for the deposit, I had to turn my attention to getting a mortgage, and this I managed through an insurance policy. Now, after three years, the loan was repaid, and almost a third of the mortgage.

During our three years there we had joined the village choir and we had got quite friendly with our rector, Bob Close, and his wife who was a teacher. We encouraged him to do without notes for his sermons – it took a long time to persuade him but he finally did manage it, and was thrilled to bits with the effect. We had a visit from the Bishop of Thetford, who had come to confirm some of the children. Bob introduced us, and said we had a healing sanctuary in the village. The bishop showed quite a lot of interest, and he paid us a visit after the Confirmation. He was very impressed with it and told Bob that he should work more closely with us as we were doing good work. He also offered to bless the Sanctuary and we had a very impressive little service.

To me the Sanctuary was rather special because the cross over the altar was of brick, and built into the wall. When we were building the Sanctuary extension we could not make up our minds about the altar. This was the focal point of the Sanctuary, and we wanted to make it look nice. I used to go to bed and dream about it. I woke up at three o'clock one morning with a clear picture in my mind of what it should be. I got up, put on some clothes, and went across to the garage. I laid out the bricks on the floor exactly as I had seen it in my mind. The bricks forming the cross stood out from the wall face by four inches. The altar top rested on two brick piers with blue shot velvet curtains draped between. Thus the whole effect was simple but pleasing to look at.

Our third Christmas there Ruth put on a Nativity play in the church. In keeping with most country village churches it was huge and freezing cold in winter. The ladies in the choir took hot-water bottles in with them to stop freezing! When Ruth started recruiting men for the nativity play, half the village said, 'Oh, you won't get him, he's much too shy to do anything like that in public,' but she roped in the most unlikely types, and they turned out tops. She had all ages from the youngest at five years old, to the more advanced at fifty plus. Everyone made their own costume, and the play was a great success, including a period when the church was in complete darkness, and the angels proceeded round the church with lighted candles.

It was agreed that we should put on a healing teach-in at Norwich for the Home Counties Association of Spiritual Healers. It took several months to organise, but we had an excellent panel of speakers including Basil Cordingly, Bishop of Thetford; Maurice Barnett, Superintendent Minister of the Methodist Central Hall, Westminster; Bertram Woods, General Organising Secretary of the Churches Fellowship for Physical and Spiritual Studies; Brother Mardus, Leader of The World Healing Crusade; Michael Bulman, senior consultant surgeon at Norfolk and Norwich Hospital; Christopher Woodard; Harry Edwards; and Gordon Turner. We also had various eminent people chairing the sessions. It was an excellent day, and did much to further the work of spiritual healing in East Anglia.

With the closure of Mallon Dene at Rustington, and our transfer of the NFSH summer school to the Overmead Hotel in Torquay, our numbers had had to be reduced from 400 to 200 because of lack of accommodation. So, to obviate disappointment of would-be students, we decided to hold one school in the spring, and another in the autumn. After our third year at the Overmead Hotel, and the success of the Norwich teach-in, we thought we would revert to a holiday camp for the summer school, and made arrangements to hold it at Corton between Yarmouth and Lowestoft. We had a very good attendance again for this, but found it a little sparse after the luxury of the hotel at Torquay. Although it was a good week, and enjoyable, we decided the hotel accommodation was generally more acceptable. The memory of this particular school is indelibly imprinted on my mind because, on the day we were leaving, I was walking past one of the rooms when I was called in by Ruth Duffield. She and her husband were vice-president and president of the Norwich Christian Spiritualist Church. She told me that she had had a message from spirit to say that I would be asked to go back to London. I was not pleased to hear this because by now we were happily settled in Norfolk. Anyway, I tried to forget about this message and to get on with my normal life.

At the next council meeting of the NFSH the question of a central headquarters was brought up by Olive Burton. She and George worked with Harry Edwards in the Sanctuary at Shere and, as the NFSH grew, so it began to take over the Sanctuary work because, when the Federation was formed, Harry Edwards had agreed to use his Sanctuary for its administration. Now more and more time and staff were being used on NFSH business, and it was time it stood on its own feet. Helen Staples took on the job of fund raising for NFSH premises, which it was agreed should be in London. Various functions were organised to raise money for this, and within nine months we were in a position to start looking for suitable premises. Albert Denton was appointed administrator designate and, with the help of Maurice Tester, found suitable premises in Gloucester Place, just off Oxford Street. These were inspected by the officers who decided they would be ideal. Then the question of staffing came up. Initially, the administrator would need an assistant and a secretary. Albert insisted there was only one person who fully understood the inner workings of the federation – and that was me. I immediately remembered Ruth Duffield's message. I refused to take the post as I did not want to return to London. Arguments then ensued for a couple of weeks, and I finally compromised by agreeing to do two days a week there only, and Albert was quite happy with that arrangement.

Things started to move – furniture was ordered, and contracts made for alterations to be made internally to suit our needs, and the date set to take over was 1 January 1970. However, in November Albert was taken ill, and any further arrangements halted for a while. Then, early in December, I had a call to go to London – Albert's condition had deteriorated and had called for an emergency meeting to discuss the future. We were snowed up in Norfolk and could not get to London. Then Harry Edwards telephoned me that evening saying the Albert was gravely ill, and was not expected to live for more than a few days – therefore I would have to take over as administrator. I said that this was impossible because I had my home and work in Norfolk, and anyway, we did not want to go back to London to live. Harry Edwards then said that it was Albert's dying wish and there was no one else who could do it anyway, and he insisted that we travel to London as soon as the weather cleared. Three days later we made the journey to London and Harry finally managed to persuade us.

Number 12 Gloucester Place was an end of terrace property, with a large basement covering the whole area of the house, and three floors above ground level. Our flat was on the top floor. Albert had engaged a secretary, whom I had, as yet, not met, so we looked forward to making her acquaintance when we took up residence on 1 January. The flat had been furnished by Albert Denton and his wife, so we had no problems in that respect, and really all we had to bring down to London were our own personal effects. We came down on the Sunday ready to start 'mopping up operations' on Monday. Little did we realise how much mopping up would be required.

There was a parking space at the side of the house, but this had been allocated to a foreign Embassy opposite which already had three parking spaces so I had nowhere to park. We had no hot water, because the tank had been taken out for replacement, and would take three weeks to arrive. The only cold water supply was in the basement and there were eighty-six stairs from the basement up to the flat carrying water. Ruth sat and wept and I swore. What in heaven's name had we let ourselves in for? Here we were, in January with no heating, windows that did not close properly, floorboards up, and mess and rubble everywhere.

The next morning we were awoken by noises that indicated that the workmen had arrived. And while I was inspecting their progress in my 'office' my secretary appeared – Phyllis Wild. The one thing that did seem to work was the telephone and Phyllis spent the first day organising plumbers, and arranging for electric fires and office equipment to be delivered. We soldiered on until Friday afternoon, when I felt we had suffered enough for one week, so Phyllis went home, and we took off for Norfolk, and the comfort of our own home.

Our restful weekend over, we returned to Gloucester Place on Sunday evening. We used the side door because the builders had scaffolding up at the front door. Having got inside, Ruth drew my attention to a dress of hers on the floor just inside the door. We were puzzled as to how it had got there and so we carried on up the first flight of stairs and, at the foot of the second flight was a locked door to keep intruders out of the office section. Stuck on the door was a note, 'Sorry, you've been burgled, get in touch with CID on Monday morning'. This welcome note was written by the builders, and the burglary must have been on Friday night. The office had been stripped bare of all portable equipment. Going on to the flat we found it in a complete shambles. The bed had been stripped off and clothes strewn about everywhere. A new electric sewing machine that Ruth had not taken out of the box had gone, also a cine camera and projector, tape recorder, and all Ruth's jewellery and personal things.

When the CID arrived the following morning we learned that eleven other premises within a quarter mile radius had been burgled on the same night. The police told us that the burglars were very professional – and also very dangerous, having cut through our telephone cable to prevent the alarm being raised. This made us very uneasy in our new 'home'. To regain some semblance of order in the office we needed a telephone, so we arranged for the engineers to come along and rewire our system. The floorboards had been replaced and, apart from tripping over paint pots, and dodging ladders, we managed to get on with what work we could until new equipment arrived. We worked for three weeks in our overcoats until a new boiler was fitted, and we could get heating re-established in the building.

By mid-January we had got the office organised, and were dealing with a daily mail of some two hundred letters. It was like being thrown into the deep end of the swimming pool without anyone there to haul you out if you could not swim. During the last week in January we had a visit from a reporter. Harry Edwards had made it known that the new headquarters would be opened on 14 February, and so the reporter had come to report on progress, and I quote from his press report:

> I called at the National Federation of Spiritual Healers' new West London Headquarters last week for a progress report. Though the interior is a shambles, conversion is well under way. Painters and carpenters, working at full pressure, have undertaken to complete the job for Harry Edwards' dedication service in three weeks. I look forward to the 'after' end product. The 'before' I saw last week was very disheartening. Healer, Gilbert Anderson, indefatigable Home Counties Association of Spiritual Healers' Chairman, is Administrator. He, and his wife Ruth, are installed in their top floor flat.

Gilbert took me on a tour of the building. We picked our way under ladders, over paint pots, avoiding newly painted walls and doors. The overall plan for this brave new healing HQ began to take shape. His back panelled offices are a peaceful oasis – in contrast to the constant traffic boom of Gloucester Place, adjacent to Marble Arch. He, and his secretary, Phyllis Wild, are already coping with massive paperwork.

The offices at the back of the building were certainly peaceful from a noise point of view, but chaos reigned supreme within I can assure you. Apart from our own work, we were constantly chasing up workmen and subcontractors, as the deadline for opening got ever nearer. Oblivious to our internal headaches Harry Edwards had sent out invitations to many influential people to attend this opening ceremony, and there looked like weeks of work yet to be completed. On 12 February the painters and carpenters were still at work. We had been let down by the curtain suppliers, and there were no carpets either. Ruth and Phyllis worked through the night making curtains, and the next day Mr Wild was also roped in to help with putting up the curtains, and a hundred and one other jobs that needed to be done. Then the big day arrived, and we still had not had the carpet delivered for the main entrance and reception area. There were more frantic telephone calls and it, and the carpet fitters arrived at eleven o'clock. A quarter of an hour before the opening it was laid and the front door opened. I do not think that anyone, least of all Harry Edwards, had a clue of what we had gone through in the first six weeks of the creation of our new headquarters. We had been blessed with the help of a number of voluntary helpers and, in addition to the normal running of the Centre, on this particular day Ruth had to convert the basement into refreshment rooms, and provide refreshments for the sixty people who attended on this special day, and she too was most grateful to those who helped to make this day a success, in spite of the many tribulations.

Phyllis Wild had been a nurse and applied for the job as secretary because, like many, she had been healed herself by Ted Fricker, the well-known healer, following nine months' medical treatment, some very unpleasant, in the hospital where she worked in the Midlands. Twelve months of travelling to London every week for treatment brought the desired result of a complete cure, and she wanted to repay her debt by working in the healing field. She was an excellent secretary, and we owed her a debt of gratitude for all the extra work she had put in during those early days in Gloucester Place.

Among the panel of healers working at the Centre were, Harry Edwards, Gordon Turner, George Chapman, Maurice Tester, Patience Denton, Karl Francis, Tom Johanson and myself. The first three months at No 12 were not all to be desired. It was almost as though some unseen power objected to our being there. For several weeks we experienced electrical office equipment breaking down for no apparent reason. Added to this, one of our best office staff had the misfortune to trip on one of the builders' cloths at the top of a flight of stone stairs leading to the cafe in the basement, and went head first to the bottom finishing with a broken hip and dislocated shoulder. It could not be said that our entry into London was uneventful, and it was a good nine months before the internal mechanism functioned smoothly.

Outside, things were different. Within two months of our takeover work started on building the Churchill Hotel on the corner opposite our headquarters. Shortly after this upheaval a new block of flats was started on the other corner and then an underground car park opposite. For twelve months we had pneumatic drills going all day and peace seemed to be the most evasive condition possible. This was the normal daytime disturbance we had to endure, but the nights were worse. It was a rare event to go through a week without some disturbance. Police sirens sounded all night long, and several times we were woken up by the police because someone had been seen on our roof. The block had flat roofs, and the only means of escape for us in the event of a fire, was up a ladder, through a small hatch with four bolts, on to the roof! There was no other means of escape, other than the eighty-six stairs. Our flat looked out on to a direct drop into an area at basement level. We often speculated what would happen if there were a fire, and we had to use this exit. By the time we had got the ladder down, the four bolts drawn, and the flap open, the flames would be licking up our behinds. After our first weekend burglary the insurance company insisted we had security locks on all doors, and I had a bunch of keys that would have rivalled any jailer. Several times we were got out of bed at night with persistent ringing of the front door bell. Ruth, by this time, was a bundle of nerves, and expected anything.

We had originally intended to go home to Norfolk every weekend but this did not last for long. Weekend functions at the Centre were being organised both to publicise it, and to raise funds. These functions we had to attend, and welcome visitors, many from overseas and, although we resented being tied down in this way, we also met some very interesting people. Quite a number of stage and television personalities came to us for help, and gave us help in return. Artists, musicians and theatrical people, will often turn to spiritual healing in preference to allopathic medicine, probably because they are more sensitive, and appreciate its value more than the more materially minded individual.

It is interesting how some people get an immediate response to healing. One lady living in Portman Square, very near the Centre, came in one day. She had been eaten up with arthritis for a number of years, with little or no respite from the pain, in spite of the masses of pills she had had from the doctor. She said, 'I honestly expect to hear myself rattle when I move, I have had so many.' All the joints of her fingers, hands, elbows, knees and feet, were very inflamed and swollen, and, although I did not say it, I thought we were not going to get very far with this one I am afraid, but I gave her healing, and suggested she made an appointment in a week's time. Next day my secretary rang through. 'There is a Mrs Bigeo on the telephone, wants to talk to you.' I thought Oh, dear, this is our arthritic patient. I wonder what is wrong?

'All right, put her through.'

'Oh. Mr Anderson, you're an angel! Do you know, all the pain and swelling has gone, and I can walk about freely without any discomfort. It's absolute heaven.'

One interesting case was a man who was suffering a lot of pain through the disintegration of the joints in the shoulders. It had got so bad that the arms dropped out of the sockets, causing excruciating pain. He had little use of his arms, and hands, which made his life additionally difficult as a theatrical manager. The cause of this problem was the result of three years' treatment on steroids gradually eating away the bone. When we met him he was unable to take any weight on the shoulders. Even a very light jacket would cause the joints to fall out of the sockets. In winter, too, he could only wear a very light cloak. He had regular healing over a period of six months, by which time he was wearing a normal jacket without any problem and, even better, was able not only to use his arms and hands quite well, but also lift and carry objects that had been completely impossible. This again was something the hospital found impossible to explain.

Another case was that of a professional violinist in a London orchestra. She fell and fractured her wrist. This was set and, after a few weeks, when the plaster was taken off, the wrist had become set, and much of the feeling gone from the fingers. She was naturally alarmed when told at the hospital that they regretted it, but her career as a violinist was finished. She had healing twice, and the full flexibility was returned to her wrist, normal feeling to the fingers, and she was able to resume her work with the orchestra.

One day I had a request from Nigeria for help. It was from The Very Reverend Worshipful David Darko Kwapong, a bishop, seeking help for his baby son, given up as incurable by the doctors. Would we send healing prayers for him? Six weeks later he wrote to say, 'Praise be to God, my son is cured.' He had just been christened 'Gilbert Anderson Kwapong'!

Syd Staples had made contact with a Dr Tomlinson in Baker Street, and we arranged to take some of our difficult patients to him for treatment – he was a homoeopath and radionic practitioner, and he, in turn, would pass some of his difficult cases to us for us to give healing. Ruth was one case that we referred to him, as her health had been a constant headache to the medical profession, and he was the only one to diagnose her diverticulitis with the use of a blood spot and the black box (radionics). We worked in his waiting room, and he was shut away in his consulting room.

One thing that intrigued us at the time, was that Dr Tomlinson had some instrument that measured the healing energy flow and, although shut away in another room, it could tell us when the healing energy started and finished, which was a maximum of two minutes. How I have wished since to have more information on this instrument. Unfortunately, he went to Australia, and died there, and we lost all trace of it. Try as they might, scientists have, as yet, failed to produce an instrument that will register this non-physical energy. The magnetic energy field is measurable by Kirlian photography on all living things – human, animal or vegetable. This is demonstrated in many ways. If a leaf is photographed on a Kirlian camera it will accurately portray the actual leaf. If a section of the leaf is cut away, and the remainder photographed, it will still show the outline of the 'missing' part of the leaf.

Professor Douglas Dean from America, has worked with this type of photography for many years, and when he was in England, he came to the Centre to do some research. I had a cancer patient to treat, and he measured the emanation from her hand before healing. He also measured mine. The Kirlian camera is unlike any normal camera – it has a flat glass surface on which the object is placed. On this occasion the patient put one hand on the plate, and I also put my hand on it. The picture was taken and it showed the outline of the hand, and the emanation from it. The patient's outline was barely visible and broken. Mine was strong and complete. This was before healing had been given. Pictures were again taken, after healing, and this time the patient's emanation was equally as strong as mine, without any lessening of the intensity of mine. Indicating the result of this 'spiritual' energy on a more physical level as it had, in no way, reduced my own physical emanation. We carried out another experiment with Douglas Dean – this time on water. I was asked to hold a small bottle of tap water in my hands for five minutes. This he sealed, and took away to test, and found that the whole molecular structure of the water had been changed by the healing energy. But still the 'before' and 'after' without any knowledge of the mystical energy 'in between' making these changes possible.

This spiritual energy is non-physical and, as yet, cannot be monitored on any of our instruments. The patient may feel heat, cold, or a mild vibration, but there will be no clinical change registered with either the feeling of heat or cold, and this can sometimes be quite intense. This can be tested by placing a thermometer between the healer's hand, and the patient's body, without any change being registered.

☆ ☆ ☆

Back at Denton there was still much activity on the healing scene generally. Being an agricultural area we had the inevitable crop spraying, with its aftermath of destruction. It was distressing to see dozens of dead birds strewn about the village within two weeks of the spraying activities. They fed on the insects, and grain, with their resultant death. We noticed our shrub lawn was being affected too, with leaves turning brown after the spraying, and it took us two years to realise that Ruth's severe attacks of what we thought of as 'flu followed the spring and autumn crop spraying. We had fields of corn on three sides of our plot, and it was plain to see the spray drifting on the wind, and it would often be carried quite a distance before settling on the ground.

When we first saw the doctor about Ruth's 'flu attacks he had said he had other patients with similar problems. I now asked him to check when these other patients had their attacks. This he did and, sure enough, they were the same times, within a week or two, according to the area where they lived, and we came to the conclusion this too was the outcome of the chemical spray. I read Rachel Carson's *Silent Spring* and found this a real revelation on the destructive effect of this chemical warfare on all forms of life. When one realised the stupidity of so-called progress, it is not difficult to see how we are digging our own graves. I made myself very unpopular with our sprayer, and many of the local farmers, by lecturing to many local organisations, particularly women's groups, letting them know just how damaging this process was. My audiences would often ask why this had not happened before the Second World War. It had not been necessary to spray the crops two or three times a year to protect them from pests. The answer was simply that before the Second World War farming was carried out in this country in a very different way. Small fields would be sown with different crops, with ditches and hedges separating the small fields and, in that way, nature kept perfect control of pests by one controlling another, and so controlling whatever type attacked that particular crop.

With the war years chemicals were produced for use against the enemy, so that, at the cessation of hostilities, that industry had to find alternative outlets. So agriculture turned to the American style of vast areas under one crop, and no pests to control the one attacking that single crop. Hedges were pulled down, and ditches filled in, so that nature was no longer in a position to maintain control, and the chemical industry continued to prosper at the expense of human life from a slightly different angle. It is interesting to see, with the passage of time, how pests are learning to combat the chemicals. The weak may be killed off, but the strong are becoming stronger, and more resistant, with the result that more spraying is becoming necessary, and more lethal chemicals are being used.

Do we ever stop to think where this is leading us? Speaking to the wife of our aerial sprayer, she said how very careful they had to be with the handling of the chemicals, having to wear protective clothing, wash every time they handled it, wearing gloves, and carrying soap and water to wash at all times when they used it. That is fine for them, but no thought is given to any human, or animal, life, that it would come into contact with. After much hard work and agitation, we did get the law amended so that all householders had to be advised before spraying started in their area, but still the destruction of bird life continues.

Lecturing in this way in the many villages and towns near by, healing would often be discussed, and we gained a number of patients as a result. One lady came over several times, for herself and one of her children. Both having responded well, she suggested to her vicar that a healing service should be held by me in the Anglican church in her village. Under considerable pressure from several other residents, he reluctantly agreed. A date was fixed, and I insisted that he took part in the service. I would give the 'laying on of hands' and he would give each one a blessing. The church was full for the first time in living memory. Patients came up to the altar rail where I gave the laying on of hands, followed by the canon's blessing. One woman had a very young baby in her arms, it had cried throughout the service, and she was feeling very embarrassed. She told me the baby had been born badly deformed, the whole right side was drawn up so that the body was twisted. I put my hands on the child and, almost immediately, she stopped crying and remained silent for the remainder of the service. After the service the canon said he had been very impressed and suggested we make this a regular monthly service. Two weeks later we received a call to go and see the baby I had healed at the service – all its deformity had disappeared.

One Saturday I had a call from Ginger Green, our boat kit friend, and Silver's owner. His son had been involved in a bad car accident, and was very smashed up. Could I go with him to hospital, and see if I could help? When we arrived and I saw him, I thought to myself, 'You might have been better off if you had been killed,' he was in such a mess. I very gently touched him, praying that whatever was best for him might be brought about. He was unconscious so there was little point in our remaining, so we left, with the assurance of the sister that she would notify him immediately any deterioration occurred. Next morning, having heard nothing, Ginger rang the hospital, asking for sister. 'How was he? Do you know it's remarkable, the boy must be made of india-rubber, he's so much better. I would never have believed it possible. In spite of numerous broken bones he's doing remarkably well.'

We had a call one day from a titled gentleman; he'd had a frozen shoulder for two months, and was getting no help from the doctor, or hospital. Could he come over, he'd had so many pills he was afraid people would hear him rattle as he walked about? He came over, and he was in a lot of pain, the slightest movement on the arm caused quite a severe pain, and, as a farmer, he needed to use his hands. After ten minutes' treatment he was raising his arm up above his head, without any discomfort. After leaving me he stayed talking to Ruth. 'Do you mind if I stay for a bit? I cannot believe the pain will not come back before long!'

'Certainly, would you like a chair?'

'No, let's sit out here on the grass by the pool, it is much nicer.' One hour later he took his leave, but not before he had asked if he could bring his wife over. She had had a hysterectomy three months ago, and still had a lot of pain. As farmers they needed to be pretty active, and this was hampering them too much. Happily, three visits overcame his wife's difficulty and we have, over the years, become good friends although we do not see each other very often now.

It was interesting to see how some people, and even families, responded so readily to spiritual healing, while others did not, and I firmly believe that we receive the blessing of healing when we are spiritually ready for it. When I injured my spine, and felt healing would not help me, I had to suffer and experience severe pain to enable me to appreciate the needs of others. Then, when I had learned the lesson, I was healed. The Bishop of Thetford was a firm advocate of spiritual healing and, according to many of the local men who had served in the Army during the Second World War, he saved the lives of many of them in Japanese prisoner of war camps, by his loving care and attention, and keeping up their spirits, often when they felt there was just nothing left in life. They were convinced, without him, they would have died.

From that first call for help, on arrival in Denton, within eighteen months we had treated over two hundred patients, with illnesses ranging from multiple sclerosis, arthritis, cancer, spinal injury, Parkinson's Disease, slipped discs, accidents, emotional problems, nervous breakdowns, mental illness, ulcers, fibroids, migraine, asthma and psoriasis. Some came from nearby towns and villages, while others came from up to 100 miles away, often making regular visits for several weeks until their trouble was overcome, or thought to be not responsive enough to warrant the long journey.

We seemed to cover Norfolk, Suffolk, fanning out westwards from Lincoln to Peterborough, Cambridge, down to London and the Essex coast. A young couple came in one day with a three and a half month old baby. When I saw them I thought it was a bit odd, both parents white and a coloured baby! They told me the child was jaundiced – I have seen jaundice before with a yellowing of the skin and eyes, but this child was BROWN. She had been born with a non-functional liver! There was no outlet from the liver, and they had been told the baby could not survive more than a few months. After a few weeks' treatment the whites of her eyes became paler, and her general colour seemed slightly better too. Five months later she went back to hospital and, to their astonishment, ducts had formed in the liver, making it possible now to link the liver with the bowel.

We had lots of people suffering from stress-related illness, particularly lady school teachers. Conditions such as asthma, bronchitis, psoriasis, migraine, and one unusual case of a boy who had suffered with ulcers in the mouth for nine years. After three treatments his mouth was clear, and remained so until he had to sit examinations at college, when they returned. Not so bad as previously, but the stress of the examinations had recreated the condition. We taught him to relax, both physically and mentally, and he had no recurrence of the ulcers, even when under pressure.

One of our rather special patients was Pat, the young lady who sang for me at the opening of the Denton Sanctuary. We first met her in August 1966. She had been bedridden with a very rare blood disease, which also caused acute rheumatoid arthritis, with very painful and swollen joints. She was unable to live any sort of a normal life and, apart from various drugs, medical help was a non-starter. She had so improved after our first visit that she was able to come to the Sanctuary for further treatment, the first time out of the house in many, many months. She came regularly every week, and each visit seemed to inject new life into her. Twelve months after our first visit to her she had had further blood tests, and her local doctor said she was better than he had ever known her in fifteen years. She was now back at work full time as a shop assistant. We still see her from time to time when in the area and now, thirty-four years later, she is still at the same shop as a senior buyer.

A man from Oulton Broad, near Lowestoft, came in with a very difficult breathing problem. He had suffered lung infection for six years, and breathing was getting more and more difficult and painful. He had his treatment, and returned the following week, saying he had had the best week in six years, breathing was easier, and he could expand his chest better than he could remember. He made four more visits, but only to say how good it was to be alive and well again.

Mrs Barlow, who lived at Thorpe House, a lovely old house just off the main road between Harleston and Diss – every time I passed it I thought what an ideal residential healing centre it would make – had a great-nephew born with a hole in his heart, a very frail, sickly child six years old. She asked if he could be put on an absent healing list for help. Several months later she rang to say how much better he seemed to be: more energy, and taking an interest in things he couldn't be bothered with before. After two years his heart had become normal, and he was prepared to fight any boy bigger than himself.

I had always loved the Norfolk Broads in the early days before it became spoilt by motor-craft, and our land lent itself to the construction of a miniature Norfolk Broads. I had a yen for water gardens, and our land was ideal for them. Behind, the bungalow was all grassed, with the highest point at the top left, falling away gradually to the right, and down to the Sanctuary. We had the main pool in front of the Sanctuary, and I planned another pool at the highest point top left – this would be one of the broads, then a channel cut representing the river, down to another pool on the right, and from this back to the main pool in front of the Sanctuary. There was a natural, gradual slope from the first broad to the second, and then back to the main pool. Water would be pumped from the main pool up to the first 'broad', then the natural fall of the land would take it round the whole circuit back to the original main pool. Miniature boat yards would be built along the 'river' at intervals completing my miniature broadland.

We got it all cut out, and ready for the pump installation and lining, when we had to go to London for the NFSH. With the increasingly infrequent visits back home, it never did get finished and what had been a beautiful garden began to look like a field of hay. At one period we had to get one of the local farmers in with his hay cutter to clear it, and the moles added to the general destruction by tunnelling all over the place. Another shattered dream!

With our increasing involvement with the NFSH headquarters I had to relinquish first my electrical business, so that all our time was given over to the healing work, and then my work at Denton itself. However, the Sanctuary continued to be used in our absence by the trainees who had developed with us during those ten years of our occupancy.

We have had some extraordinary experiences with animals and their supersensitivity that I would like to tell you about. 'Carlo' the golden retriever we had before the Second World War, in addition to his quick response to air raid warning instructions, and involvement with the Army sergeant-major, already mentioned, had another sense that we found strange.

When we first moved to Wymondham in Norfolk, it was difficult to cope with the dog too, so we left him with Ruth's parents in North London. About three weeks later we decided to drive down to London to see her parents. It was done on the spur of the moment, and we didn't leave Wymondham until nine in the evening not telling them we were going. We arrived at eleven-thirty and, strangely, they were not at all surprised at our unexpected arrival. When we mentioned this Ruth's mother said, 'Oh, we half expected you because ever since nine-thirty Carlo has been backwards and forwards to the front door, and he's never done it before!' Strange? But they kept him for several months, and every time we went down he always knew, and gave them due warning with his restless pacing to and from the lounge to the front door. Sadly, we lost Carlo during the early years of the War. When we both joined up Ruth left him with a friend at Upminster. Several months later this friend wrote saying they had *lost* Carlo. We found this hard to believe because he was so well-known in the district. We contacted the police and vets with whom Ruth had worked in her ARP for animals duty. They made extensive enquiries, but he was never found.

'Jimmy' was a mongrel to whom I got rather attached during our transport business days. I made regular weekly calls on poultry farmers, collecting their eggs to go to London. One farm, a few miles out of Kings Lynn, was set back off the main road by about half a mile, with a private road leading down to it. On one visit I saw this dog sitting at the side of the road leading down to the farm. As I turned into the farm road Jimmy jumped up wagging his tail – all two inches of it – and barking. I stopped, opened the cab door, and up he jumped, and rode down to the farm with me. This became a ritual every Thursday, and only Thursday. He would take up his position at the top of the lane, and await my arrival, and we became quite good friends. After about three months the farmer said, 'Look, Jimmy has taken a real shine to you, would you like to keep him? I've got too many dogs anyway!' So I took him home to Wymondham. After a couple of weeks Ruth said, 'You know I love dogs, but Jimmy irritates me. He spends hours every day with his nose glued to the back door, and that stupid bit of tail going like mad. If I let him out heaven knows where he will go, and I can't spend all day taking him for walks, he's never satisfied.' After a while he settled down a bit and, as Christmas was on hand, we were going to spend it with Ruth's parents. On arrival there we warned them of Jimmy's urge for the wide open spaces, and not to let him out. We were netted all round the garden, so that he could move freely within those confines, and got down to the festivities. Christmas Day and Boxing Day came and went, and time for our return to Wymondham. All packed and ready to go. Where's Jimmy? A search of the house and garden resulted in no Jimmy. We had to get back for work next day and, after telephoning the local police, left it to Ruth's brothers to let us know when he turned up, and we'd get down as soon as we could, and collect him. One week, two weeks went by without a whisper. The third week I made my customary call at the farm, near Kings Lynn, and who should be sitting at the top of the lane? Jimmy!! I had taken him from West Norfolk to East Norfolk in the lorry, he'd stayed in Wymondham for nearly three months, when we'd taken him from there direct (at night) to London where he'd never been before. Somehow he had completed the third side of a triangle completely off his own bat to his original home. What unique homing device do they possess to enable them to do such perfect navigation in unknown territory? Needless to say we left him back at his farm home, and he continued with his weekly rides down the lane quite happily. He obviously was used to an outdoor existence, and did not enjoy being restricted for long.

'Silver', the steeplechasing horse that had been saved from being put down by our friends in Norfolk, earned himself the reputation of troublemaker. Whenever there was a large gathering of people and horses he would somehow entice half of the competing horses away into other fields, either by nuzzling open the gate, or jumping the fences. Little Shelley, who was then nine years old, has been married for several years now, and is the proud possessor of over two hundred rosettes won by him in local events. He even ran away with her in the early days of his rejuvenation. He enjoyed twenty years of extended life with their thanks to spiritual healing and their care.

'Tara' was a black cocker spaniel with the most beautiful nature. She was Ruth's shadow, and they were inseparable.

When she was in season we had problems, she was so prolific. We had to resort to putting her in plastic pants, to protect carpets and furniture, and I have never seen an animal react more like a human in all my life. She hid herself away from everyone, and looked absolutely disgusted that we should degrade her in this way! After a couple of years, we spoke to the vet about it, and she advised a hysterectomy, which we agreed to. Tara was always welcomed at the surgery because she was so good, they could do almost anything to her, and she wouldn't murmur. She had the operation and, shortly after, Ruth was talking to a neighbour about it, saying how very quickly it had healed, with very little to see. She turned Tara over to show her, and from then on we only had to mention the operation to anyone in her presence, and she would roll over on her back and 'show her operation' very like a lot of people who invite others to 'see my operation'.

We had a driveway leading to the bungalow and, when Ruth went out in the car without her, she would take up her position on the driveway, lying there facing the road, watching the occasional passer-by who would invariably stop and talk to her. From Longfield, our bungalow, turning left would take us to Bungay, and right to Harleston. After a while Tara would change her position, and face either right, or left, instead of straight ahead. I didn't think anything of this for a while, until it occurred to me that every time she was facing in the direction that Ruth came back from. To us this was pure speculation because she could just as easily come in from either, and it was often half an hour or more, before Ruth appeared that she had taken up her position. How did she know? It never failed in fourteen years.

One of the villagers, a farmer's wife, who was in our developing group, rang us saying one of her kittens had been run over, and broken its back. Would I go over and have a look at it? I went along and it lay there, could only move its head. I spent a few minutes with it, and advised if it wasn't any better in the morning to take it to the vet, and he would put it out of its misery. She rang next morning. When she came downstairs the kitten was halfway up the curtains, leapt from there on to the table, and flying about as though nothing had happened.

At one of our summer schools in Torquay Ruth contracted

a serious kidney complaint, and was too ill to even remember the journey home to Palmers Green. Billy, our matron friend, insisted she went straight back to her house at the hospital, and the doctor said she should be in the ward. Billy insisted she was better off with her, between us we could manage with the odd nurse coming in from time to time. Billy had a red cocker spaniel 'Beauty' and for four days while Ruth was delirious she would not leave the foot of her bed. We had to drag her off to do her 'jobs' and she was straight back again. Billy apologised to the consultant for the dog being on the bed, and he said, 'She is all right where she is, leave her there, they know where they can be of most help!'

'Blue boy', our budgie, used to stay at Billy's if we were away for schools, or anything similar, and Rosaria, her Italian maid, was a fresh air fanatic. One weekend she had the window open all night by his cage. He caught pneumonia and died. We buried him at the foot of an apple tree near the lounge window. This had been grass for as long as anyone could remember. Next spring, one daffodil bloomed from that very spot where the bird had been buried. It had not been there before and no human had put it there!

9

RESEARCH, REMOVAL AND RIVALRY

In 1971 the NFSH council decided to research into spiritual healing, and see if any instrument could be found that would register this non-physical energy. A symposium for parapsychology research was held at our headquarters in May, with researchers from many fields in attendance, including six doctors, two professional electronics engineers, six independent researchers and representatives from CFPSS College of Psychic Science, De la Warr Laboratories, Hygea Studios, Belling Lee, Birmingham University, Truth Research Foundation and ourselves. In addition to those attending this symposium a further eight doctors expressed their deep interest in our findings.

At a further meeting in June the research committee was formed comprising Professor W M Tiller and Dennis Fare as joint chairmen, Richard Gargan, Harry Edwards, Olive Burton, John Findlay, R A Bontoft, Marcus McCausland, the doctors Mary Austin, Maxwell Hall, Ian Pearce and Hunt, and myself. It was also agreed that the healing experiments with Harry Edwards would be in three stages. Firstly, to identify the parts of the body being affected by healing, using individuals who can see the aura (*vide karagulla*) or aurameters or kilner spectacles – whichever shows greatest reliability. Secondly, working in a Faraday cage, to measure, with the acupuncture system connected to the healer and patient, the points and areas which should be investigated and measured on the individuals. Thirdly, to connect healer and patient to whatever instruments were available to give read-out of responses at various levels so as to show cause and effect of healing using meters, graphs, photographs, etc.

At our second meeting it was agreed we should concentrate on a special illness, or disease and, as cancer was the most feared disease of modern times, this was to be our focal point for research. Firstly, we needed to prepare a questionnaire that would give us the information we needed, much of which would be of a very personal and intimate nature and, with the help of some of our doctors, we produced a very comprehensive 142 question paper to send out to 1,000 cancer sufferers. Having printed the questionnaire, we then turned to finding the patients to send them to and, to our amazement, out of the hundreds we knew who had cancer, only a very few had been told by their doctors, or consultants, that they actually had the disease. We anticipated, once this questionnaire really got under way, that a lot of work would be involved in extracting the required information and, once again, fate seemed to play a part. A colleague of the NFSH chairman had severe back trouble, which had not responded to either a medical corset or traction. He came for healing and, with one treatment, was completely free of pain. It so happened he was head of a very large group of companies' computer department and, in appreciation of our help, put their computer system at our disposal, without charge.

However, months went by with just a trickle of the questionnaires coming through, so this valuable service had to be shelved, at least for the time being. Although this was disappointing, there were always plenty of things to keep me occupied, one of which was our Annual Bazaar. This was a two-day function supported by the membership, affiliated associations and many friends, and it was so gratifying to see the vast amount of goods, and money, that came in for us on these occasions. These were always well advertised, so we had visitors from many parts of the country attending. Harry Edwards, of course, was there, and would always draw a large crowd. One of his daughters 'Bunty' painted many oils for us to sell, and these were always extremely popular. Over these rather hectic two days we used to average £1,000 clear profit and, remembering that we were a charity, existing solely on voluntary contributions, this was one of our greatest survival efforts.

Administration took up most of my time, although I would have preferred to be healing but, as compensation, Ruth and I had the pleasure of entertaining many interesting people and giving them tours of inspection of our headquarters. It was on one of these tours of inspection that a crack in the wall was pointed out to me. This was on the side wall of the house and, when I had time to examine it later, found it extended from the top floor down to the basement. This gave me some feeling of disquiet, and so I asked the advice of one of our members who was in the building trade. Remembering all the building that had gone on nearby over the previous eighteen months, I envisaged the wall coming apart. We stuck paper strips over the cracks at intervals on the various levels, and we kept an eye on them to see if there was any movement over the next few weeks. Within three weeks the paper had split indicating continuing movement, so I called in the surveyor. On inspecting our cracks he was quite alarmed and pointed out that because it was a 'listed building' at the end of our lease we would have to leave it in perfect order. Our crack continued to open and so we started looking for alternative accommodation.

Several weeks went by while we searched, but without much success. Then we had a property offered us outside London. It was a lovely old manor house with a small amount of ground and old coach house and car park at Loughton, Essex, near the underground station direct to London, and on a regular bus route between London and Epping. The NFSH council inspected it, and it was agreed we should buy it, provided we could sell Gloucester Place. We never expected to sell, but within twenty-four hours of it being put on the market, the estate agent had come up with three interested buyers. And so the trauma of London's West End was coming to a close, and we looked forward to a more peaceful existence in the outer perimeter of London.

I remembered Loughton as a youngster when we used to cycle out to the Epping Forest from Palmers Green, but it bore no resemblance now to what I could remember of it all those years ago. It was then a small hamlet on the edge of the forest, but now it was a busy commuter area in the executive belt of outer London.

'Shortacres', our new headquarters, was at the top of the hill out of the town going north to Epping, and consisted of four floors, including a large attic flat above ground level, and a basement, plus an outside boiler house, and lovely old coach house, with the stalls still intact at one end for four horses, and the open area for housing two coaches. It stood at a crossroads, with pleasant lawns and trees facing the main road, and the car park and coach house entrance in the side road which led on to the forest. It was a quite imposing house of character and had, prior to our taking it over, been an old people's home for a number of years. We learned it had originally had very extensive grounds, which had been built on bit by bit over the years as the town had developed.

Another advantage from my point of view was the fact that it was north of London, and saved us the tedious journey out of central London when we had the chance to get home to Norfolk, cutting the journey time down by nearly an hour. Once again our residence would be at the top of the house but, taking a longer view, we had other ideas that were much more attractive. The coach house was L-shaped, and had great potential for conversion. I could already see it in my mind as a detached residence, near to, but away from, the headquarters building.

The great day came for our removal. Two articulated lorries arrived at Gloucester Place, and spent all day loading all the equipment, furniture, and what seemed like tons of paper work, ready for delivery to 'Shortacres' next day. Most of our staff were coming to Loughton with us, and I had been able to recruit some additional local help too. And within two days of moving in to Shortacres we had got ourselves organised and all systems working satisfactorily.

Not long after moving in I had occasion to go down into town and, among other things, I bought the local paper *The Loughton Gazette* and was intrigued to see the front page headline in bold black type 'The Devil moves into Loughton'. My immediate thoughts were 'Good Lord, what have we come into?' and read on with considerable interest, only to find out that we were the Devil and I was his number one disciple. I found this rather breathtaking, as we had only just arrived in a strange town, unknown as far as I knew, to anyone, and we were already front page news. The article was written by a Pentecostal minister who reminded me that we were not welcome in Loughton.

On my return to Shortacres I came face to face with the

Anglican parson who lived in the rectory opposite. I asked him if he agreed with those sentiments but he said that their author was 'rather a fanatic'. And apparently while we were in Norfolk the previous weekend he and a band of his followers were outside our gate singing hymns and praying for our souls. He had wanted to get into our grounds but the police would not let him.

Several weeks of crossfire in the local paper resulted from this article, and we agreed that the best thing to do was let the people decide for themselves. Harry Edwards would give a public demonstration in the Town Hall, and the local people could decide for themselves whether, or not, it was the healing love of God manifesting, or the work of the Devil, as our Pentecostal friend was trying to convince people.

In view of this attack, and the publicity, I wrote to all the clergy representing the various denominations, inviting them to be our guests at the demonstration, and suggesting, as we had one common purpose – healing the sick – it might be to everyone's advantage if we had a meeting, so that we could work together for the common good of the community. We also invited all the doctors to attend and, if they wished, to sit on the platform, and examine the patients before and after healing, so that they could see, at first hand, the changes taking place by these natural phenomena. One local doctor telephoned, saying he would very much like to attend, and asked for two tickets. He telephoned again a week later saying his colleagues had advised him to get the approval of the BMA Ethical Committee to attend and examine the patients being treated, and now he was forbidden, not only to examine the patients, but even to attend the meeting. I learned later that he had attended incognito, was very impressed, and his wife became a patient of ours for a time, with satisfactory results. In fact, I had a very good working relationship with three doctors, one later as a patient, and the other two in research. The response to the proposed meeting with the clergy was better than I had expected. Eight wrote saying they would welcome a meeting, and this was arranged at the presbytery, with the Catholic priest as chairman. We had a very fruitful two hours' discussion, and I was given the floor for well over an hour, talking of our work, and answering questions. At the conclusion, it was agreed we should have another meeting inviting other clergy to attend from further afield. The general summing up of this first meeting was that we should hold healing services in the church, with healers and clergy working together.

The second meeting came along and, to my surprise, some fifty people attended, with representatives from the lesser known groups, and the Church Army. Another very healthy discussion took place, and I was feeling satisfied that we were, at last, in tune with the various denominations in relation to healing. The Catholic priest, having chaired the meeting again, called on one of the Anglican priests, who had been conducting healing services in his, and other churches, to sum up the meeting, and his summing up was simple and effective. He said, 'Much as I admire Anderson for what he thinks he's doing, it's obvious, as he works outside the church, he is working with the Devil.' That closed the meeting, and any further hope of continuing the good relationship we had been building up.

One thing that the healing demonstration did, however, was to establish Shortacres as a much appreciated healing centre, by not only local people, but also many who came long distances for help. The two members of staff who had survived the move from London were Eileen Hambling, my secretary and the wife of the late well-known medium, Horace Hambling, and our receptionist, Gina Rhodes. The remainder of the staff was made up from local people. Healers still gave their services freely, coming from many different areas on a one-day-a-week basis, and Harry Edwards gave us one day a month for healing appointments.

After we had been at Loughton for eighteen months, Ruth and I decided to have a week at Torquay for a break. Overmead did not take dogs in the normal way but, when we had our schools there at the end of the season, we took over the whole hotel, and Tara, our black spaniel, was always welcomed. We did not want to take advantage of the kindness of the Manager and Manageress, Mr and Mrs Codman, so took a flat in Paignton with the dog. On our second day we drove into Torquay and up to Overmead to see Mr and Mrs Codman. We had Tara out on the cliff top, opposite the hotel, and a couple got into conversation through the dog. 'Are you staying at Overmead?' they asked.

'We wanted to bring our dog, but they won't take them. No, we are friendly with the manager, and have come up to see them. We are staying in Paignton. Where do you come from?'

'Loughton,' was the reply.

'Good Lord, so do we.' We exchanged addresses, and what we were doing, and they belonged to an Old Tyme Music Hall Company, the Loughton Players.

'You must come along to one of our rehearsals, we have lots of fun.' We had coffee in the garden, and I went inside to see Leonard Codman.

'Hello, what are you doing here?'

'Oh, we're staying at Paignton with Tara.'

'Nonsense, you will stay here, at least during the day, in our private apartment. We cannot offer you a bed because we are full, but you must come here during the day.' This was very good, and we spent most of the week with Bill and Margaret, our new-found friends.

About three weeks back home, and Margaret rang to say there was a rehearsal the next evening. 'Why not come down and meet our producer and some of the gang, they're a grand crowd.' So we went along, and they certainly did seem to get quite a kick out of what they did. They put on shows in hospitals, old people's homes, for disabled and even mentally retarded and blind people, which I found hard to appreciate, until I actually saw the tremendous enjoyment those handicapped people got from them. We got plied with questions. 'What can you do? There must be something! You used to be in a church choir! Well, that's just the job.' Ruth mentioned my Red Riding Hood epic at Booker, and we were in head first.

Quick changes were sometimes a riot, we even had to change behind the piano in one place, often changing rooms no bigger than a cupboard but, in spite of all this, we enjoyed every moment. We all preferred it when we could get down among the audience, and get some of them involved in our antics, making it more enjoyable both for us, and for them. With the blind, they would have someone who described what each player was wearing, and generally acting as their eyes.

All this was a complete contrast to our everyday work, and a very welcome break, as well as adding to our repertoire for the last night concerts at the annual schools. We had about twenty members in the Players, and we all had several individual numbers in addition to the concerted items, so that we could put on a three-hour show almost at a moment's notice, if necessary, and everyone had a fair chance of doing their bit fairly regularly, if they wanted.

The headquarters was now nicely settled, and working smoothly, with one exception. Several of the staff, either refused to go into one of the rooms on the office floor, or felt uneasy when they did, and we decided there must be a presence there – probably one of the early residents, or owners, of the house, in the past. Ruth, and one of the staff, had seen a shadowy figure of a man of slight build, dressed in frock coat and top hat, but his influence was not one of agitation, rather of annoyance at being disturbed. The room upstairs, however, had a very different feeling, one of great agitation and distress, and this was making it difficult with some of the staff. Two of our members often did exorcism with earthbound souls, and we asked them if they would come over and see what they could do to clear this condition.

They came along, and the wife who was a medium, invited the entity to take her over, and her husband would talk to them, and explain that they were no longer living on the earth, but had moved on to a higher life in spirit. The first spirit was the man Ruth had seen, and he said he was the owner of the house, and resented the intrusion of all these people into his privacy. He still lived there, but no one seemed to take any notice of his requests for them to leave him in peace. He was told he had passed on from the earth life, and there were people there with him to show him the way to his new life. He thought that was rubbish, because he had always been taught that when you die there is nothing more – you are dead, and he could not be dead because, here he was talking to them.

Lengthy discussion ensued explaining to him that it was only his physical body that had died – his spirit, the real eternal inner part of him, lived on free of the confines of the physical world, and there was a wonderful life waiting for him to experience in this other world. He was told to look behind him, and he would see a friend who was waiting to lead him on into this new life. He thanked our friend, and went contentedly on his way, and we did not see him again.

Then the disturbed influence was invited to take over the medium, and she explained she had been a maid in the house, had fallen in love with one of the manservants who had gone away and left her pregnant. She was very distressed because she could not find him. Again, her circumstances were explained to her, both she and her baby – now grown up in spirit – would be cared for, and loved, if she would accept that she had left the earth condition, and a new life was waiting for her. She was told to take the hand of the person at her side, and she would be shown the new and exciting life that awaited her. She too moved on, and the whole atmosphere of the house resumed a calm peace that we all felt and enjoyed.

I found this form of exorcism so very refreshing and instructive, because these possessing entities are usually those who have been taught that when we die we stay dead, until the final trumpet sounds, and we all go to heaven, or hell. These people are still human beings like you and me, who need to be re-educated into the reality of so-called after life, which is not after life, but the continuity of it in a slightly different form.

I am saddened when I hear of the forceful ejection of these possessing spirits by orthodox clergy with their form of exorcism, with no regard to how these ejected spirits are going to take up their occupation again, still thinking they are living in the material world, and must have a physical body to manifest through. What a pity they will not take off the blinkers of narrow teaching, and do a little honest researching into what to them is the forbidden unknown – the true reality of the continuity of life.

Around this time we decided to convert the coach house into living accommodation for Ruth and myself. This meant stripping out the whole of the inside before any work could be started, so I decided to make a start myself. I spent most of one Saturday tearing down the linings of walls and ceilings. At the time I was reminded that we had had a complaint of overhanging branches on the side road of our property, and the police wanted it seen to so I went out, and spent an hour or so, cutting back to keep the footpath clear. I felt the cold wind on my back, having got very hot with my indoors work, but thought nothing of it until next morning when I attempted to get up. I got a terrible searing pain in my back, and I was unable to move. This was the start of three months' hell in bed. On the Monday Ruth called in the doctor, who prescribed some pain killing drugs to cope with the pain – the slightest movement was agony. By Tuesday evening I was vomiting every few minutes. Ruth called the doctor again but he was not in, so she called another doctor friend of ours, told him what was happening, and he agreed to come over straight away. As soon as he saw me he diagnosed that I had drug poisoning and gave me something to counter the effect which, happily, reacted fairly quickly. For two months I was incapable of doing anything for myself, and I ran the NFSH headquarters from my bed. Then we had a council meeting when it was necessary for me to be present. We had a folding camp bed in the council room and, having crawled slowly downstairs, I could lie on it, and work from there. Half way through the meeting a question came up concerning some papers which were in my office. I sat up and got off the camp bed with no pain or restricted movement, for the first time in three months. I had been next to Harry Edwards and, all he had done physically when we started, was just touch my knee, and say, 'Take it easy, you'll be all right' and, here I was, walking quite freely, and able to sit in a chair without pain. But I did learn a lesson not to do things that would aggravate my old spinal trouble.

During my period of inactivity, work on the coach house was going on apace. Ron Buckle, our builder friend who was also a council member, had roped in another Ron to help. He was Ron Brooks, and he was a general handyman about the place, and seemed to be able to turn his hand to anything successfully. So the two Ronnies had really got cracking during my period of inactivity, and it was beginning to look a treat. It was L-shaped, with the main structure comprising the lounge, with sliding doors, through to the diner/kitchen, an open pine staircase from the hall up to the bathroom, toilet and two bedrooms. Altogether a very attractive and comfortable home, with a patio at the side should we wish to sit out in the evenings, or weekends.

Our pentecostal opponents had given up their fight and, all in all, life was flowing nice and smoothly, everyone minding their own business, and seemingly happy.

Then we met up with a young man, Don Player who, with his mother, had taken over a big house at Epping – just on the edge of the forest, as a home for mentally handicapped adults, to get them out of hospitals, and help them contribute something useful to society. We liked this, and helped wherever we could. I became a trustee, and we watched these people being taught to do something useful with their lives. They would garden, help with laundry, packing sweets, and other items, for local firms, and really enjoying doing something, instead of sitting sedated, day after day, in a hospital ward. It was good to see them beginning to come alive. We would help them with garden parties, and many other forms of fund raising from which they got a lot of enjoyment. They were lovable characters, and we were always sure of a welcome when we went to see them.

One of our council representatives from Liverpool wanted to put on a school in Blackpool, and asked if Ruth and I would direct it. We had a very pleasant week there and among those attending were a number of members from the continent – Germany, Switzerland, Holland, Belgium and Austria were represented. I suggested they should form a Continental Federation of Healing. I agreed to let them have names and addresses of any of our members in their countries, and they would try and get them together towards the formation of this Federation.

Out of the eight members present, the only one to take real action was Herbert Ziemer in Germany. He wrote to me six months later saying he had got a group of thirty people together who wanted to form a Federation in Germany. They had a small castle where we could hold an inaugural meeting to get them started. He asked if I would bring someone else with me, and have a teaching seminar there in conjunction with the inaugural meeting. I took Diana Craig and we had a very pleasant and productive few days at Schloss Schonic. The castle was owned by a delightful lady, very sympathetic to our aims, and I was particularly impressed with their private chapel. The castle had been in the family for a very long time, and her grandfather had painted a picture of Christ, with outstretched arms, covering the whole of one wall above the altar. It almost took your breath away when entering the chapel for the first time it was so beautifully done. This was the start of a very strong and healthy German Federation of Spiritual Healers, and annual teaching weeks in various parts of West Germany were attended by four hundred, or so, participants.

Anni Ziemer, Herbert's wife, was the principal of the German Federation, and its healer, and two other women, who gave a great deal of time, both as interpreters and lecturers, were Anneliese Gleditsch and Rotraut von Carnap.

Ron Buckle, our builder friend, was the next to be recruited for lecturing and teaching out there, and Diana Craig, who was able to go over more frequently than I, did a lot of lecturing and teaching tours with Rotraut von Carnap and Anni Ziemer, spending several weeks in the year over there.

On one of my individual trips with Ruth, we spent one week with Herr and Frau Ziemer doing healing every day in various parts in the Bonn area, and meeting some interesting people, and visiting a most unusual church, one built on top of another. It was called a douple church, and the centre of the floor of the upper church was open, and one could look down into the lower church. The object of this type of building I could not find out, but I could see little point in it myself. From Bonn we were going down to Munich to spend a week with Dr and Anneliese Gleditsch, but had been asked to stop off at Karlsruhr to heal some horses. We spent the night there as the guests of Gunter Sierek who owned the horses, and his mother, and Ruth and she had quite a hilarious time conversing in sign language.

Next morning, after breakfasting together at our hotel, we said our reluctant goodbyes, and went on to Munich. Dr Jochen Gleditsch had a medical consulting room in Munich and took us along to see it. I was very impressed by it. I had previously visited an acupuncture clinic in Bonn, and a dental clinic in the same town and, here again, in Munich, you could have been in one of our principle teaching hospitals, their equipment was so far advanced to ours. We had not thought of laser treatment then, but they had been using it for several years, with considerable success.

The one thing that impressed me most with these teaching trips to Germany, was the tremendous enthusiasm of these young people in particular, to learn. They would travel long distances to attend a school or seminar on healing and alternative medicine.

Then, with great expansion of the NFSH over its first twenty years, it extended into fifty-eight countries, and so it was suggested that it should be changed to an international organisation, with a few of us opting for a closer link with all the healing arts. At a special meeting to discuss this change, many believed we would lose our national prestige built up over its twenty years, and others were against removing the word spiritual from its title. It was finally resolved that the National Federation of Spiritual Healers should retain its own identity, but sponsor the formation of a World Federation of Healing. At the end of 1972 notice was sent out to all members worldwide, asking for their comments, and over four hundred letters came back enthusiastically agreeing to the proposition. The World Federation of Healing was inaugurated at Westfield College, London, on 5 September 1975 with Dennis Fare as President; Rev Belding Bingham (USA) Vice-president; Harry Edwards, Hon Vice-President; Gilbert Anderson, Secretary General; and John Findlay, Treasurer. Council representatives elected were from Holland, Iceland, the United States and the United Kingdom. At the inaugural meeting fourteen countries were represented and, in four years, this representation had grown to thirty countries.

Conferences have been held in London, Canada, Holland, Australia, South Wales and York, with Germany anticipated in 1991, and these are its principles:

1. The World Federation of Healing seeks to unite all practitioners in the healing field into the recognition of the holistic approach to health. Recognising that all creatures exist on a multi-dimensional basis – ie. Body, mind and spirit. That disease may result from disharmony in any of these areas.
2. It seeks to establish harmony and cooperation between all branches of the healing disciplines to enable each to use its own particular skills to the maximum benefit of the sick in mind, body or spirit.
3. The Federation aims to cut across the barriers of language, race or culture by drawing together under one umbrella exponents of all disciplines of healing from

whatever race or background they may come, to assist individually and collectively in promoting world awareness of Man's spiritual nature and its reflection on bodily health and happiness.

4. It seeks to draw into membership all qualified practitioners whether allopathic, homoeopathic or other alternative therapies such as acupuncture, osteopathy, psychotherapy, chiropractic, radionics, herbalism, naturopathy, diet, healing, etc. It aims to alert the public to the existence of these various disciplines and to guide and encourage their responsible use in cooperation between practitioner and patient.

5. The Federation aims to educate the public to their responsibility for their own health. To knowing that in addition to receiving treatment they can help themselves from within through the greater use of the natural resources.

6. The Federation will promote all aspects of the holistic approach to health by providing a platform at meetings and conferences for the different disciplines to be lectured upon and discussed.

7. It seeks to maintain and improve standards of practice and competence of practitioners in all disciplines of healing and to identify and expose any incompetence or malpractice found to be detrimental to the high standard it has set.

8. The Federation seeks to be a bridge to enable individuals of all the healing disciplines to join together into the one organisation so that by closer cooperation as individuals or through their respective organisations they may widen and improve their service to the cause of world health.

9. The Federation will work to secure the passage of legislation by the United Kingdom and European parliaments which will recognise the alternative professional practitioner and healer.

10. The Federation welcomes the more liberal attitude now becoming prevalent within the British Medical profession and will alert other countries and the public to the conditions under which medical practitioners may cooperate with non-medical practitioners and healers

without fear of disciplinary action.
11. The Federation seeks to offer the knowledge and research of the world to aid the less developed countries and to encourage the use of alternative therapies, especially where medical aid is limited.
12. The Federation will seek to cooperate and promote research programmes. These will be mainly concerned with the ways in which the holistic aspect of health can be achieved by wider public understanding and education. The research into specific diseases will be considered when the level of the research fund allows this.
13. The Federation will encourage the compiling of National Directories of Healers.

Elected presidents to date have been:
1975   Dennis Fare
1977   Dennis Fare
1978   Christopher Woodard
1979   Ian C B Pearce
1981   William T Jones
1983   Marian Butler
1985   Mary C Brierly
1987   Gilbert Anderson

10

PSYCHIC SURGERY

Resulting from our efforts to research into healing, and my trips to Germany, we had a visit from two German doctors. They were a husband-and-wife team from Frankfurt and they had just returned from a visit to the Philippines, where they had taken some of their patients who had defied their medical knowledge and skill to overcome their illnesses. They had taken them to the well-known psychic healer Tony Agpaoa for help and they had brought along films of this controversial form of healing.

Sigrun Seutemann the wife, had a most interesting story to tell. The year before, they had read of the work of Tony Agpaoa, and had taken a group of their patients out to see what he could do for them. While working on a patient, he had turned to Sigrun and said, 'I want to treat your heart.' Nothing had been said about any disability with her, but she had been born with a heart defect, and exertion for her was extremely painful, so she had geared her movement so that it was not noticeable to others. Medically it was an incurable condition, and both she and her husband accepted it as such, so that comment coming from Tony was quite a shock. He was a psychic surgeon, and could penetrate the body, and remove diseased tissue, or tumours, without any form of instrument or anaesthetic. When the time came for her operation, her husband asked if he might photograph it. Tony said yes, but he must be very quick because the heart was a very delicate organ to expose to strong light in this way. He got the camera ready and, when he saw the chest opened, and the heart exposed, he dropped the camera in surprise. Tony told Sigrun that her heart was out of place, and that she would feel a slight discomfort as he corrected it. It was all over in two or three minutes, after which she could breathe normally, and move about freely for the first time in her twenty-eight years. Whereas hitherto she would have to pause half way across an ordinary room, due to pain, she could now walk and run without any discomfort. Because of this dramatic change they had made up their minds to take as many very sick patients as they could to Tony for help, sometimes even at their own expense. They showed me the film, and I could readily accept this form of psychic surgery having been involved earlier with similar phenomena myself.

They spoke to our officers saying I should go with them on their next visit to decide, on behalf of the NFSH whether or not this was genuine or, as many would have it, a fake and a form of sleight of hand. It was agreed that I should go. It would be a ten to fourteen day visit and I was to stay with them for three days prior to taking off. Sigrun met me at Frankfurt airport, and we went to their home a few miles out of the city. She asked if I would like to spend the next day in their surgery in Frankfurt, and I readily agreed. We retired rather early I thought, at nine o'clock in the evening, but I found out why next morning when I was called at five-thirty for breakfast, and at seven o'clock they started their day's clinic, and this went on until eight o'clock in the evening, six days a week, unless they were away on one of these Philippine trips. They certainly did not shy away from work. We got home, had a meal, and set off on a long drive to Lake Constance, where we would spend the night. It was near midnight when we arrived, and I was quite ready for bed, but Sigrun amazed me, still as full of life as she had been sixteen or more hours before. The next morning, while I had a tour of the lake, Sigrun held another surgery for about thirty patients.

Then it was midday and, after a hurried meal, we were on our way to the airport, and it was a revelation to see Sigrun with the patients – forty-five of them, all classified as incurable by medical standards. She was here, there and everywhere, getting them together and organised. The last patient to arrive was a stretcher case who came straight from hospital by ambulance. When I saw him settled in the aircraft he looked dreadful, and I could not see him making the journey alive. I spoke to Sigrun about him, and she was confident that if we could get him there he would be fine. We had a twenty-four hour flight to look forward to before reaching Manila, then another flight up into the mountains to Tony's home at Baguio City. We had four stops to refuel *en route*, and I was thankful for the chance to stretch my legs, and I could not imagine how some of these very ill people were coping, but I am sure their last hope of possible survival must have made this tedious journey more bearable for them.

One incident I found interesting to break the monotony of the flight, was provided by a young girl. At our first refuelling stop I walked down the gangway to leave the plane for half an hour and as I walked down I felt a pull on my sleeve. Looking round I saw this child gazing up into my face. I spoke to her but, getting no response, went on my way. At our next stop I had forgotten the incident until exactly the same thing happened again. I tried talking to her without any response, so I turned to her parents who sat beside her. They did not understand English, nor I German, so again I moved on. Each time we stopped and I left the aircraft this same procedure took place, and I got more and more intrigued by this child. She looked to be about eight years old, but there was something appealing about her that I could not define.

Finally, we arrived at Manila, and it was like walking into an oven from the aircraft. The coach taking us to the hotel for our two nights' stay before going on to Baguio City, filled up, and three of us were left to make our way by taxi. On arrival at the hotel, the first person to greet me in the foyer was this young girl, who took me by the hand, leading me through into the lounge, indicated a seat for me to take, trotted off, and came back with an ice cold drink for me. By now we had an odd relationship building up. I talked to her, and petted her a bit, but all I got was this strange look in return. The mere fact of being able to do something for me seemed to give the child great satisfaction, and so this strange relationship grew. Next morning I came down to breakfast to find my little companion standing at her table. As soon as I sat down with some Swiss doctors I had met, she came over, held up her face to be kissed, then went happily back to her table, and got on with her breakfast. This was the pattern both at lunch and dinner, and it looked really like a mini romance developing. I had to know more about her, and asked Sigrun what was her reason for being with us. She seemed very healthy to me. Then the tragic story was revealed. When she was fifteen months old she had been injected for smallpox, and this had resulted in total loss of hearing. She was now nine, and for nearly eight years had lost one of the greatest blessings one can have. She had never learned to speak because she could not hear. My heart went out to this little soul, and I almost wept at the thought of her complete isolation. From that moment I felt very privileged that she should have singled me out from so many others for her show of attention and affection. My feelings for her now were magnified with love and compassion, which I tried to convey with her constant visits to our table at meal times.

At dinner on our second day we three, the two Swiss doctors and I, were talking about the healing we had seen done by Tony that day, and the remarkable things that had happened. Isabella, our little friend, was standing by me, and I had my arm round her shoulders, when one of the doctors drew my attention to her – her mouth was moving as we talked, as though she was taking part in the conversation. Then a sound came from her mouth, followed by a startled look on her face. She put her hands over her ears – took them away – and a look of utter surprise came over her face. She was hearing for the first time in nearly eight years. We were both amazed and delighted. She had come out to be treated by Tony, and she had not seen him yet. I began to see now why she had been attracted to me. Like the mentally retarded children at the St Neots home, she had sensed something in me that could benefit her. Once more I was reminded of the true simplicity of healing – its essence is love and compassion, these feelings had been uppermost in me for her, and the healing had taken place without any actual effort on my part. As far as I was concerned, she was here for Tony's help, but it had happened in this unusual way. Naturally, I kept in contact with the family, and she went to a special school for a time, and made excellent progress with her speech and learning.

For two days in Manila we watched fascinated while Tony and one of his assistants performed their unusual form of psychic surgery. It was rather like a conveyor belt system. He would have a patient on the bed (he used an ordinary bed in the hotel bedroom, with a plastic sheet to protect the bedclothes), he would ascertain where the trouble was, open the body, do whatever was necessary, and the whole operation would be over in about three minutes. Then the next one on, and so on. This went on for hours non-stop.

Let me try to explain what I saw. With many of these psychic healers the work is done in a trance condition. Tony, however, had progressed beyond this state, and worked on a mental attunement with his control. This was evident when, during an operation, his hands would be deftly working inside the patient's body, and he would turn his head away to talk to us. This form of control, we know, is rapidly replacing the trance work of the past, as we move forward to a finer form of mediumship.

His day would usually start at eight o'clock with a list of some forty patients. He would have one assistant who was training under his guidance, who would round up the patients, and see there was no delay. The patient would be helped on to the bed and, according to where the problem was, only that small area would have to be uncovered. No stripping off because there was so little blood disturbed. I asked why there was so little blood flowing when the body was opened, and this was all part of the process. Mentally Tony can stop any flow of blood to the area that is opened, while it remains open, so that only the blood that was there would be disturbed with whatever had to be done with the operation then, as soon as Tony's hands were taken away, the opening immediately closed, without any indication of scarring, or any mark to show of having been opened.

To start, Tony's control would tell him where to enter the body of the patient, and this was not always at the seat of the pain which might be reflective, but always it was at the point that needed attention. Then his two hands would gently massage over that area for a few seconds then, almost quicker than the eye could see, the body was open, and the tumour, or whatever the problem was, clearly revealed. Although I could readily appreciate this form of surgery, I still found it hard to believe that the patient felt no discomfort, and would often be holding a conversation with Tony about anything but what was going on.

A plastic pail would be placed at the side of the bed to take whatever had been removed from the patient. A number of medical and television teams had been out there, and said all of this was faked. Sometimes he would use cotton wool dipped in water to help with his penetration of the body. The sceptics' theory of this was that he either had anaesthetic in the water, or it was impregnated into the cotton wool. I was there to investigate these various allegations, and satisfy myself, on behalf of the NFSH whether or not there was any truth in them.

On this count, I went into town, and bought my own cotton wool, to replace theirs, emptied the bowl of water, and refilled it from the tap (due to the monsoons and flooding, the water has to be boiled before drinking, it is so badly contaminated – one of our doctors went down with poisoning just by cleaning his teeth with tap water) and did everything I could to break down these theories. Throughout the whole day I had Tony in view all the time he was working. He went from the bed after each operation to the wash basin to wash his hands, back to the bed for the next patient, never out of my sight, and changing water and wool made no difference whatever to him or his work. It was also alleged he had animal tissue hidden on his person, and made out this was taken from the patients. With the high temperatures, he wore a short-sleeved silk shirt and light trousers only. By the end of the session he would have two or three buckets full of tumours and other matter he had taken from patients – quite impossible, therefore, to hide anything on his person, no matter how vivid an imagination one might have.

Another theory put forward was that the body was not really opened at all, it was just made to look as though it was, and the fingers were folded back to give the impression that the body had actually been entered, and always that the abdomen, and other soft parts of the body were worked on, where indentations could easily be made making it look as though an entry had been effected. However, I saw over thirty operations on spines where there is no soft tissue at all, with equal success.

After two days in Manila we flew up to Baguio City to Tony's centre. This had been built for him by a wealthy American grateful patient. It was on the side of a mountain, with his operating theatre and chapel on the lower level, and his living accommodation above. The operating theatre was built with a balcony above around the walls so that visitors could watch him working. Knowing that I was there to investigate, he offered me every facility to film and take part, whenever possible. The patient who was so ill on the journey but did make it, was one of the first to be attended to. He had fourteen tumours in his stomach, with four of the major ones removed at the first operation, with three further operations to follow at two day intervals.

With everyone seeming to enjoy their operations I felt the need to be able to go home and say – yes this is quite true – I have experienced it myself. So I asked Tony if he would open my body during our stay, so that I could say, without fear of contradiction that it happened to me. This was agreed, and on the fifth day between patients he said to hop on the couch and he would do my back. I had not mentioned it to anyone but, sitting in the one position for so long on the flight, had caused me some pain in the form of a continual niggle, which had been a bit wearying. I lay on the couch on my stomach for maybe two or three minutes when he tapped my shoulder saying it was all over. I didn't think he had even touched me and he showed me some gritty substance on his fingers, together with a little blood. The doctors also confirmed what he had done, but I still was not satisfied, and asked if he could do it somewhere where I could actually see it next time. He said he would try, time permitting.

One day I was in the gallery filming when Tony called me down to help him with a man who was paralysed from the waist down. We got him on the couch, Tony at his head, and me at his feet. We stood there for a few seconds, then Tony told me to touch the man's feet. As my arms went forward to touch his feet, I felt a tremendous surge of power flow down my arms and, as I touched his feet, his knees bent, and his feet shot away from me. We repeated this three times, then Tony told the man to get off the couch, and walk round the room. And he did just that, with a light touch on the couch for his balance, and he really was elated. Then Tony told me to take him into the chapel, and finish off with my kind of healing, which I did. The man left me a pair of crutches as a memento.

Before coming on this trip I had seen several professionally-produced films of the psychic surgery and, in every case, it was not possible to see a tumour actually being removed as there was always a hand screening the actual removal, so I tried very hard to get a film of this actually happening, and I was fortunate in capturing on film a tumour taken from the thyroid of a patient, showing it very clearly.

One operation I would dearly have loved to film was a young boy with a brain tumour. Unfortunately, the electricity supply in the Philippines is very erratic and on this particular day there was no power, so filming was not possible. This lad was about ten years old, and had a shock of black curly hair and, to get to the tumour, it was necessary to penetrate the skull. Here again, Tony started with a light massage movement on the scalp then, not only was the flesh opened, but also that part of the skull dematerialised showing the brain and tumour clearly exposed. I wonder if you can imagine my feeling of disquiet while watching hands poking about in someone's brain, and taking out the tumour while looking at us, and talking about what he was doing. This again bore out my theory that his hands were controlled by a much higher intelligence but, at the same time, was fully aware of what was going on around as well. I could imagine some of those curly locks getting trapped when he took his hands away, and the skull and scalp closed, but it was just as though a fine toothed comb was controlling it – not a hair was disturbed, or misplaced.

The doctor who had failed to film his wife's heart operation, asked if he might try with someone else. The father of the little deaf girl, who had attached herself to me, had a heart condition, and Tony agreed, provided it was quick. With heart operations Tony worked under a towel because of light having an adverse effect of the phenomena, so it was a quick flip back of the towel, flash taken and covered again. This was the only case, out of over five hundred operations, that showed any mark after the opening closed, showing a red scar mark for several months, presumably from the flash light.

The man who had the abdominal tumours, had a stomach that felt like a pebble beach – hard and very uneven. On his third operation I was invited to take quite a large tumour from his stomach. It was the size of a large Victoria plum. I took it in my hand but it would not budge, then I saw Tony's hand pass over the body, roughly two feet above, and the growth immediately came away as though it had been cut out, and my hand had been inside his stomach, there was no question of fraud or imagination. Of the five hundred or so operations that I saw, or took part in, which were on eyes, ears, noses, throats, brains, lungs, hearts, nerves, paralysis, abdomens, feet, spines and deformities, with about forty per cent there was a major improvement resulting, and the majority feeling varying degrees of betterment.

One morning Tony took me to the lowlands to see one of his colleague's work. We had a rather tortuous two and a half hour journey down mountain roads half washed away in places – the monsoon rains are so prolonged and severe it is not worth repairing many of the roads. We finally arrived at his 'church' which was an erection of breeze blocks and tin roof, with openings for windows and doors, and an earth floor. When we arrived we found about one hundred natives there with all kinds of sickness, some having walked many miles to get help. One thing I quickly learned was that you were either quite rich, or very poor, in that country. The natives literally lived off whatever they could find growing in the ground, and their lifestyle was very meagre indeed.

The healing started with a religious service, then the healing followed. The healer had a plain folding trestle table for his operating couch, but first he gave injections for various conditions. The patients filed along about eight feet away from the healer, who pointed a finger at them, and they moved on. I asked him what was going on, and he said he was giving psychic injections. When I queried this I was told to join the end of the queue, which I did, and when my turn finally came, he pointed twice, and I felt two sharp pricks on my upper arm and, looking later, there were two red spots where I had felt the injections. He had a most unusual form of diagnosing. One of his helpers would hold up a white towel in front of the patient, and the healer would be able to see the seat of the trouble. It was rather like an X-ray, except that we could see nothing behind the towel, but he got an X-ray picture through it. At one juncture he turned to me, and asked whether I knew anything about witchcraft. I said I didn't but he showed me a woman who had been cursed with pain, and she had been unable to get relief from it. He opened her abdomen and took out a five-inch long chicken feather with a sharp quill. Whoever had cursed her in this way had dematerialised the feather, and rematerialised it inside her. Was it fake? No, I still have the feather as proof, and she went away a very happy woman. In these rather remote islands witch doctors still practise and psychic surgery has developed from it but, like most things we learn to use, they can be used for good, or ill.

While we were in the lowlands Tony took us to the place where he was born, and we met his parents. It was a very primitive hut built up on stilts, about four feet above ground level because of the flooding during the monsoon periods. Just a plain wooden hut, with a shelf round the walls on which they slept.

We 'dropped' in on one or two of the lesser known healers in the lowland areas, just to see how they managed. They were natives, very poor looking after their neighbours, just a rough wooden couch, but always a Bible was used as a headrest, and we learned that their form of development was much the same as ours. Starting with automatic writing, progressing to trance healing and diagnosing, ultimately moving on to the mental attunement practised by Tony and some of the more advanced healers, and so ended a very interesting and instructive day among the poorer people of the island.

One evening we visited a village a few miles out of Baguio City where the natives made and sold their wood carvings, and it is amazing what they produce with mallet and chisel – some of the most beautiful carving I have ever seen. Life-size figures of men and women, in perfect form, even to the rippling muscles of the men. Sadly, it would have cost more to get it home than the actual cost of the figure. I did, however, bring home some beautiful work carved out of what they call monkey fir, a lovely knot-free mahogany coloured hardwood. It was most interesting to see the natives working at the roadside in their open workshops.

President Marcos had a summer palace in Baguio City, and his daughter-in-law spent a morning at Tony's centre when we were there. There was an old monastery at the highest point in Baguio which overlooked the city below, and it was interesting looking down seeing how rich and poor seemed to rub shoulders with the modern buildings of the wealthy against the shacks of the natives. The two doctors I had travelled out with had set up a trust to buy the monastery, and convert it into a residential healing centre, with Tony as its principal. Three days after the healing of the paralysed native, Tony was standing by the window waiting for a patient who was rather slow on her feet, to come for treatment, when he called me over. He pointed out of the window and I saw the man who had been paralysed climbing a flight of sixteen stairs without any difficulty or assistance.

Later that day there was another slight lull between patients and so Tony said he would open my leg. I was on my back with my slacks pulled down to my knees. He moved his hands gently over my thigh, and then there was a slit some eight inches long where I could clearly see bone, sinew and muscle, without feeling any discomfort at all. It was quite remarkable seeing inside my leg, yet feeling nothing but surprise. As soon as he removed his hand from the opening it closed almost more quickly than the eye could see, and not a mark on the skin to show for it. I could now go home and say that I had not only seen these phenomena, but also experienced it on my own body, and watched it happen. I had done everything possible to disprove the accusations of fraud, and there was one last item to cover. It was said that the matter taken from patients was not human, but animal, so I had to bring samples home with me for analysis and, not only did they prove to be human, but they also matched the blood of the patient in each case.

I was quite satisfied that of the five hundred or so operations I witnessed during my ten days with Tony, everything was perfectly genuine, and functioned under natural law. My filming resulted in a forty minute colour film, showing many of these psychic operations, the people and country, and the conditions under which they live. The regular showing of this film raised several hundred pounds for our research programme. I asked Tony what the chances were of a European developing this form of psychic surgery, and he said that in my case, if I had spent a month with him, I would be doing it. This was because I had earlier been involved in other forms of psychic phenomena.

We discussed their form of healing, and realised it was developed basically for the Filipino people who were uneducated by western standards, and needed to *see* something manifest before they would accept its reality. Looking back to our early days of mediumship, it was similar in so far as people needed physical phenomena in this country before they would accept the reality of these little known powers. Physical mediumship was quite commonplace then, but now, with people's understanding broadening, it is no longer necessary to prove these energies – they are more readily accepted by the majority of thinking people. Tony's view was that, within about twenty years, they too in the Philippines would be healing in much the same way as we do in the United Kingdom. No longer will it be necessary for them to prove the powers any more. I remember reading that only two years before my visit in 1970, there were 'head hunters' still found in some of the outer islands, indicating the primitive type of individual they were dealing with.

I think it is obvious why doctors and television crews discredited this back in this country. Can you imagine the trouble that would be caused with and by the medical profession if we advocated it here, and frankly, apart from the spectacular aspect of this form of healing, it achieves no more than our simple natural 'laying on of hands' and prayer? The Filipino receives benefit from healing because they 'see and believe'. We in the western world have learned to benefit from it because we believe in the love of God from whence this power flows, and we privileged ones are just a means of transmitting it in love and humility.

I look upon my trip as a privilege as it enhanced my understanding of just how little we really do understand of the wonders of our universe and the true nature of life. Three of the paraplegics did not respond physically from Tony's help, but they were happy and contented when we left to go home, so I feel they were helped on one of the more subtle levels such as mind, or spirit, while others, with similar conditions, were able to walk after treatment. I wonder if this bears out my belief that we receive healing when we are spiritually ready, because I am sure there is much to be learned through sickness and suffering and when we have learned we receive that blessing.

The majority, however, made the return journey in a much happier and healthier state, and I feel sure that they too had responded because they had not progressed beyond the state of needing to see disease taken out of their bodies before they could accept that it would work. I began to realise that our thoughts do have a bearing on our lives and health.

When we had decided to research into spiritual healing I had been drawn to looking more deeply into why we became ill, and this entailed an in-depth study of people's habits, attitudes and general behaviour, to see if there was any connection here that might throw light as to 'why'. Looking back over patients' records, particularly those with serious illnesses, it was very revealing that emotional problems played quite a large part in their lives, and it is astonishing how many people carry these burdens, so I made a study of clinical psychology and psychotherapy, and learned a tremendous amount from it. It gave me a greater depth of understanding of people and myself. I began to appreciate the saying 'God helps those who help themselves', and that the cooperation of the patient would speed up the healing process. We are looking at spiritual healing in its truer sense, healing the spirit and the more subtle levels of our existence, like thoughts and emotions where the bulk of our physical ills have their origin. In this way we are learning to bring all of these energy forces together, mind, body, emotion and spirit, which make up the complete being, so that we see the person not just as a physical being, but as a whole person. For years we have tried to convince the medical profession that this is a complementary therapy which should run harmoniously alongside allopathic medicine. We are each healing on completely different levels, both of which are vital to the wellbeing of the patient.

We often think about spiritual development on our own account, but not so much for those who have moved on to the next life. This was brought home to us one Christmas when we met at Billy's home with some friends. We had our usual Christmas group seance and, among those speaking through me was a very cultured, educated voice who introduced himself as Richard Troutman. 'You won't recognise me, but if I were to . . .' here he gave a shrill whistle, '. . . say it's Ginger, you would remember me.' This was the cockney boy who had come to prepare our physical circles at the church years ago! He then told us a very interesting story. When we closed the physical circle he was very fed up because he had enjoyed these meetings, and was now left with nothing to do. When we opened our own Sanctuary at Palmers Green he 'looked in' with a view to having some fun. He watched patients coming and going, seeing some remarkable changes in many of them, and forgot what he had come for completely. After several visits like this he decided he would like to be involved in this work and told White Eagle (who was one of my helpers in spirit) of his wishes. 'You realise what is involved, don't you, you will have to go to school, and study very hard for quite a long time.' Yes, that was all right, he wanted to do that, and was quite ready and willing to learn! So, he had gone away, and we had not heard from, or of him, for several years. He had been to school, and college, finally specialising on the brain and mental sickness. He had come to tell us he had just passed his final examinations, and was ready to start working with me. Was it coincidence that, without knowing anything of this, I had been drawn into the study of psychology, and mental and emotional illness? I think not. I have no doubt that our pathway is shaped for us by higher intelligence, and we are led to do these things when the time is right. The transformation of Ginger, the cockney boy out for a lark, to this well-spoken, educated and knowledgeable Richard, was quite a revelation to us all.

I had a call one day, or rather a command, from an actress to go to her flat in Kensington without delay. She was in pain, and I had to do something about it. On arrival it was rather like bedlam. She was walking backwards and forwards about the room, shouting orders to another woman with her, and her pet parrot was screeching its head off. I discovered she had trigeminal neuralgia – not a nice thing to have at any time, but we had a touch of melodrama thrown in for good measure. She was an interesting lady, but her word was her command, no matter who was involved. After my third command to her presence, I heard no more, so assumed all had returned to as near as normal as she would allow.

I mentioned earlier that we had an annual re-dedication service at Mr Edwards's Sanctuary, Burrows Lea, near Guildford and, on one of these occasions I wanted to take a cine film of the proceedings, and he suggested I went up into his mother's bedroom, which was an ideal position from which to film. His mother was in her nineties and very, very deaf, but a charming lady. Halfway through the proceedings she came into her room and objected to my being there. I tried to explain what was going on, and her son had suggested I use her room, but she could not hear, or understand what I was trying to impart and, pushing me aside, went to the window and in the middle of our guest speaker's talk to the two hundred-odd assembly, called out, 'Henry, come up here at once, there is a man in my room!'

With our infrequent visits back home to Norfolk, things were getting neglected; more often than not when we decided we would have a weekend at home, something would turn up to prevent it, either a visit from someone overseas, or a meeting that we had to attend, with the result that the garden, which had once been my pride and joy, was beginning to look rather like a jungle. The ornamental pond that had contained about forty fish, was getting overgrown and, on one of these visits, I decided to give it a good clean out. Having got rid of much of the unwanted plant life, I found all of the larger fish had disappeared, and only small ones remained, nothing bigger than three inches long. The last time I had seen them the original ones had grown to nine inches but now they just were not there. My immediate reaction was that some of the local children had been helping themselves. I asked a neighbour if they had seen children in the garden. He said, 'No, why?' And I told him of the missing fish. 'Ah! That explains it then, we have noticed herons visiting your garden regularly, and wondered why. They have been taking your fish.'

One of our near neighbours was a good friend, both he and his wife were Norfolk born, and he had an electrical shop in Bungay. He was a great entertainer by telling stories in full Norfolk brogue, of incidents that had occurred with the business. In a nearby village some of the cottages were being converted to electricity from oil lamps for lighting. One of his men had been out there doing the wiring and, three days after it was completed, the woman came into the shop complaining, 'They dang ol things baint no good, boy, the ont light up.' He said he would send a man along to put it right. When he got there he was shown the various light bulbs, and they were all black! He asked her what she had been doing, and she had been trying to light the electric bulbs with a candle! Another lady had bought an electric food mixer, and you can guess what – she had not fitted the top properly, and her vegetable soup was spattered all over the walls and ceiling!

Jan had attended a funeral I had taken for one of Ruth's brothers, and she told George, when either of them went, I was to do the honours. Two weeks before his death we were having coffee with him and, instead of his ridiculing death, and life after death, as was his usual custom, he said, 'I had a most unusual dream two nights ago. I was at one of my daughters' houses, and yet I was not there. A strange feeling of being there but not being there.' This was the first time he had ever been serious about this kind of thing, and he wanted us to say what it meant. I forget what we did say at the time, but two weeks later he dropped dead with heart failure. I am sure he felt he was nearing the end of this life, and was looking more seriously at the situation, because he said, 'You know, Jan has got it all arranged that you will take my funeral!' And, this time, unlike him, he was not joking about it.

In 1964 I was invited to open a new Spiritualist Church in Potters Bar, and Dr Paul Renault, my control, dedicated it to Spirit, and the service of mankind. Last year I returned to celebrate its twenty-fifth anniversary and as always, the church was full because, in keeping with all Spiritualist churches, healing plays as important a part as the proof of survival after death, and spiritual philosophy.

On the days that Harry Edwards came to Shortacres, Tara, our spaniel, would go missing. After lengthy searches she would be found in the healing room with him, either sitting, or lying, by his side. When at first they called her away, he said, 'No, leave her there, she's all right,' and she would stay there for hours quite happily. At other times when he was not there, she would take up her position on the chair facing Gina, our receptionist, that was intended for patients when they booked in. She was a very good judge of character too, if she did not like someone she would emit a low growl of disapproval and, sure enough, they would prove to be unpleasant people. From her position in reception she knew when patients were going into the healing room for treatment, and often she would beat them on to the healing stool! The healer would tell her to get down but, more often than not, the patient would say, 'Oh no, let her have hers first. I don't mind!'

11

WHAT THE HEALERS SAY

In 1973 I had a visit from an American journalist, Sally Hammond, who was over here to do a survey of British healers and, after a long session together, she left with enough material to keep her busy for quite a long time. She wanted to contact as many of our healer members as possible, and get a general survey of how, what, when and why they became involved in healing. We decided the easiest way, and probably the best, was to produce a questionnaire of all she wanted to know, and circulate it to the members, and this is what she did. The rest of this chapter is her summary of the work which ultimately led to the publication of her book *We are all healers*.

In England, members of the royal family, members of parliament (MPs), symphonic maestros, operatic tenors and business tycoons go to spiritual healers for treatment. The reason for their confidence is that many of Britain's healers have banded together in an unique 4,000-member society called the National Federation of Spiritual Healers which upholds high ethical and professional standards. To belong, applicants must provide proof of their healing ability, take the Hippocratic Oath just like doctors, and complete prescribed study courses. Adding to their prestige is recognition by the government's Ministry of Health of the right to treat patients in 1,500 National Health hospitals, with the approval of the patient's doctor (only one doctor, in a mental hospital, has so far balked at the ruling!).

What more can America's growing numbers of aspiring healers learn from these experienced Britons aside from the great advantages of organising? To find an answer, I sent out a long questionnaire to a sampling of rank-and-file healer-members of the NFSH, with the gracious cooperation of its administrator, Gilbert Anderson. In forty questions I tried to discover how they first got into the field, their methods of developing the healing gift, types of healing they do, religious backgrounds, guiding philosophies and so forth, and in the months following I received 150 endlessly fascinating replies, one of the first coming from Britain's most famous healer and the Federation's president, Harry Edwards. Here was a representative cross-section of Britain's spiritual healers, many practising in remote countries and villages with two or three on the Channel Isles of Jersey and Guernsey and in Scotland as well as varied corners of London – all members of the first and only healer's union in the world.

Combining the information they gave me with that given me 'live' by several of the more widely known healers, I put together, I believe, a fairly well-rounded picture of spiritual healing in the first country where it has acquired the momentum of a 'movement'. Much of it appears in my book *We are all healers* (published by Harper and Row), in a large section entitled 'England as a laboratory'.

About half of the healers took the time and thought to write detailed replies on separate sheets, and many thanked me for having asked their help. The impression came through of a heartwarming group of people with the highest spiritual motivation, out-going, humble, ('I am only a channel', they say over and over), whose intense desire to ease all kinds of suffering had become a way of life. Their patients were not only human but dogs, cats, wild birds, rabbits and foxes. And many reflected keen intellects and mellowed humour as well as spiritual awareness.

During my research trip to England I had gathered from conversations with average Britons that, while wonderfully tolerant by nature, they considered spiritual healers somewhat offbeat, and I wondered how they could maintain such an offhand attitude towards this beautiful natural resource in their midst.

The most striking aspect of their replies was the fact that so many had astonishing and sometimes eerie experiences that led them into the field of healing. There was also a surprising number reporting that doctors sent them patients and sometimes came for treatment themselves. Here are some general findings.

According to the sample (1,000, of which fifteen per cent responded) Britain's spiritual healers are predominantly male, by nearly two to one, and four per cent are husband-and-wife teams. Most of them discovered their ability to heal in their thirties and forties, but they might have begun healing at any age – from five years (by healing their pets or mothers' headaches) right up to a ripe seventy-one.

They come from many walks of life and professions, including a London police constable, a lawyer, a retired Army major, a one-time opera singer, a Church of England rector's widow, a retired civil servant, a tailor, an ambulance driver/attendant, a one-time manufacturer, an accountant and a district manager of an assurance company. One woman described herself as 'a perfectly normal housewife and mother of three teenage children'.

Two-thirds of my correspondents said they heal in their own homes, often in a room or annexe set aside as a sanctuary. An equal number said they also heal in the patient's home if very ill or bed-ridden. Forty per cent heal in churches, often a little Spiritualist church in the neighbourhood. Less often they work with others in spiritual healing clinics, hospitals, hired halls and public demonstrations. One healer wrote, 'In my home, in the street, any place!' Many said they work at everyday jobs and see their patients evenings and weekends, and a good many expressed a yearning to be able to quit their jobs and heal full-time.

In reply to Question 1 ('In what manner did you discover that you had the ability to heal?'), Miss Marian Butler of the Temple of Light sanctuary in Swansea, Wales, told this story:

> I discovered I had the gift when my nephew suffered from encephalitis, was paralysed, unable to lift arm or leg, totally blind, deaf and dumb. Through strong prayerful intercessions, caused powerful energy to enter the bedroom, and in a matter of fifteen minutes saw that his speech, sight and hearing had been restored completely. He was then

three and is now twenty-five, enjoying good health. I decided to investigate what had happened, went to a Christian Spiritualist Church and sat in a development circle regularly. I have gone from strength to strength and now treat hundreds of patients each month.

A E Phillips of The Healing Brotherhood, Hemel Hempstead, Hertfordshire, is one of several who said they were encouraged to develop their healing gift by Harry Edwards.

> I took my wife to Mr Harry Edwards. Her turn came and she sat before him. He knew neither my wife nor me. He ran his fingers down her spine, then turned to me sitting some fifteen feet away, beckoned to me and told me she had a curvature of the spine. I knew this. Medicos had told her so. He spoke and said, 'Would you care to heal this?' And when I declared it was impossible, he took my hands, looked at them and said, 'You have healer's hands. Place them over that part of the spine.' I did as requested and he put his hands over mine, told my wife to bend to the right, and to my surprise, the spine moved back into place! His advice to me was to now go and join a healing group, which I did.

Miss Hetta Bowskill, of Arlesey, Bedfordshire, said she had always loved looking after the young and the old. Then twelve years ago she was told at church that she should develop her gift of healing. She believes she saw a vision of Christ:

> On my first healing, I was being used for a lady who had a growth on one side of her face. I was caught in a beam of light and it seemed to me I was struck by lightning. Then a tall figure of beauty, colour pink and blue, appeared. The eyes were the life-giving substance from which tears flowed. Never have I seen such love and compassion. I had to sit down. The lady was completely cured.

William Cross, of Brentwood, Essex, was convalescing after removal of his right lung when he was 'recruited':

> I was in a weak state. I began to see people I knew were just not there, but they were talking to me . . . I soon began to know their names. Among them were a Greek brain surgeon and a man who called himself a 'master healer' . . . One day a woman came into my office. Her face was wracked with pain. I asked her what was wrong. She answered, 'Migraine'. She had had it for years. I said, 'Do you believe I can help you?' She looked at me and said, 'Yes'. We communed together and I asked our Father God's help. She was healed within the hour. Later, a back condition of thirty years' standing was cleared up and lumps in her chest were reduced and disappeared. I had completed my first healing.

George E Gay, of New Malden, Surrey, saved a life apparently, the first time he attempted healing:

> My wife and I were on our way to Holland to tour the bulb fields. Ten minutes before the plane was to take off, she collapsed. The airport doctor diagnosed heart attack and sent for an ambulance. Awaiting its arrival, she said, 'Please don't let me die'. I said, 'Don't worry, darling, I won't'. And for the first time I tried spiritual healing, invoking the aid of God. After waiting some hours in the hospital, the doctor came out and told me they were all very puzzled. While her heart was not all that it should be, it was in no way bad enough for such a severe attack. He proposed a few days observation in an intensive care unit. After a week I was told she could come home as nothing wrong could be found. She has had no trouble since.

Phyllis Palmer of Swansea wrote that she discovered her ability to heal when her little daughter collapsed of a spinal sinus.

I heard a voice say, 'Heal thy child', she recalls, and, feeling impressed to place her hands on the child's head, she did so and her daughter recovered.

The late Reverend R A Bontoft de St Quentin, of Frinton, Essex, reports discovering his gift 'at the sudden recovery, to my surprise, of a lung cancer case in extremis – still living with no recurrence after sixteen years.' (An Anglican minister for over forty years, he describes himself as 'a Christian free-thinker'.) Londoner David Hadda began developing his ability seven years ago after a child told him his hands were 'fizzy'. And Dennis Mitchell, of Plymouth, saw a vision of his dead grandmother who clearly told him he had the gift of healing.

Question 2 ('Describe your method of developing your healing gift') revealed that many lost no time signing up for NFSH study courses or those given at the Spiritualist Association of Great Britain in London's Belgrave Square. They also studied healing from books – many mentioned those of Harry Edwards – and many joined psychic development or healing groups, often at Spiritualist churches but also in private homes, where they practised meditation, healing prayer, and attunement. Some typical comments:

> Kept sitting for twenty years for unfolding of healing gifts. Now, spiritually, I get literally filled with healing power. It seems to flow out from all parts of me. I have made great progress. First, heal the mind, and through silence, prayer, and uplifting one's thoughts, we come into Higher Consciousness.

> Above all I practised healing toothaches, headaches, most complaints. The more I practised, the stronger it became and the more my faith and belief came.

> Regular meditation and attunement made me acutely aware of spirit helpers.

Gilbert Weyell, of South Woodford, London, 'began research work privately into the immense realm of the human psyche and its interrelationship with the physical, its supernormal powers and abilities, its control (conscious and unconscious) over both physical and mental health,' while Geoffrey Dauscha of Andover concentrated on disciplined living habits. H C S Warne sat in a trance circle where instruction on healing technique was given from the spirit side of life by 'spirit doctors and healers', he said, and Barry Weekes noted that he and his wife Joan supplemented their study courses, finding 'inner peace through a guru'. Margaret Rushforth added:

> One always tried to make the next act of healing the best because one is never good enough. More prayer before and after, more concentration, more love given to God and the patient, as well as improving the use of the psychic faculties involved.

The types of healing they do? Question 3 brought out a wide variety. Nearly all said they practised the traditional laying on of hands, and nearly half combined it with prayer healing. Less than one-third said they did absent or distant healing and about twelve per cent, magnetic healing, in which the healer uses his own bodily energies rather than psychic energy channelled through him. These were by no means all. In the category marked 'other' they wrote 'massage, spiritual conversation, herbal remedies, manipulation and soul healing.' Three or four said they did psychic surgery. Listed also were somno-therapy (inducing a light sleep, then giving the patient the laying on of hands), trance healing, colour healing, the use of 'healing pads' to make contact in absent healing, and Holy Communion, confession and anointing with oil, to name but a few.

Question 6 asked the healers to give their own theories on what causes healing and how it takes place. Some expressed their view simply, others expounded at length. Geoffrey Dauscha took the view widely held in England that while healing comes from God, He uses many doctors, nurses, and others who were gifted healers on earth but are now in Spirit as His 'healing ministers' or agents:

> There are many rays, radiations and forces put into this world for the benefit of humanity. Scientists on earth have as yet very little knowledge of their existence. Spirit doctors have had the opportunity of studying the effects of these rays for medical purposes. They have been taught how to harness and convert the properties of these radiations, etc., to help restore to health the sick bodies of man . . . Owing to the higher frequency of the spirit people and the high frequency of the many rays which are used for healing, the healing medium's body is somewhat as a transformer to bring both down to a lower earthly frequency. The medium's hands direct the rays and enable the spirit doctor's hands to work underneath them, ie. to operate, adjust and manipulate as necessary.

Major McDermott, of Bude, Cornwall, offered an alternate theory to the above which he considers an 'oversimplification' in view of some aspects of psychical research:

> First, we have the subconscious healing power which automatically attacks disease and heals physical lesions. This acts – without any effort of the conscious mind – with such immediate appreciation of the special needs of the moment that it might even mean that a superior mind is activating it, and the question arises, of what or who this superior mind is?
>
> Now, the records of psychical research, eg. in Myers' *Phantasms of the Living,* are cases which show that the spirit inhabits the body here and now and is capable of acting on its own initiative without the knowledge of the conscious mind to which it must be superior. Could it not be possible that the spirit of a healer such as Harry Edwards, after the refining influence of years of devoted service to others, might be capable of carrying out the healing process without any help from spirits no longer in the flesh? When, eventually, the time comes for him to leave

this life, no spiritualist would express any surprise if he were found – the very next day – to be the spirit in charge of a healing. Why, then, should his spirit not be capable of doing this now? It is interesting to note in this connection that when questioned on a television programme some time ago he stated that though he believed that the doctors Lister and Pasteur were his guides when he started healing, he no longer consciously contacted any guide when healing.

Victor Harold Child expanded on the foregoing while focusing on the phenomenon of absent healing. It is caused, he says, by 'any or all' of the following:

> (a) By stimulation – or speeding up – of the patient's own healing capacity, whether by the healer's own healing guides and/or the healer's own positively directed and clearly focused thought. The latter is significantly strengthened by an inner conviction of God's unlimited power to heal, especially when invoked in the name of Jesus Christ 'believing'.
> (b) By the direct application by spirit guides or spirit groups. Or by the healer (acting as a transformer), of at present unknown rays or frequencies which modify or alter the sub-atomic energy structure of diseased tissue or growths, thus changing the nature of such tissue (diseased to healthy) or eliminating it altogether (growths disappearing).
> (c) By good – influencing the patient at soul level to remove any existing causes of psychosomatic illness (eg. long-held negative emotions, such as hatred, etc.).
> (d) In the rare cases of possession, the actual vocal 'casting out' of the invading entity in the name of Jesus Christ (see Mark Chapter 9). This exorcism should only be undertaken by those who have had, or are convinced they have had, an authentic vision, or visitation, of Jesus Christ, or of the Christ Spirit in their own lives and have remained dedicated to their Heavenly vision.

Frank Cook, of Northwich, Cheshire, sees a special protective role for the Spirit Doctor in the healing process:

> Power, all power, comes from Almighty God, is used, but not consumed, and can be used again indefinitely. Like a motor car, it knows neither good nor ill, and as a car can be used for good, it can also kill, depending on who has control of it. The Eternal Spirit will release power when asked, and the healing spirits use this power to heal. Thus it is kept in the right hands, not let loose where a dark spirit can gain control of it for the wrong uses.

Speaking for the many, although a minority, who prefer to think in terms of the Holy Spirit rather than spirit doctors – possibly only a semantic difference – was the Reverend J Russell Moston, whose religious background is Methodist:

> The Holy Spirit is the agent, using a healing power which is within each individual and all around us. The Holy Spirit is in control of this power. The healer is but a channel.

Others put their understanding of the healing process more briefly:

> The body is sick only when the soul is sick. One has to go about changing the thought pattern and making the soul pure. (Mrs M T Forster, Northamptonshire)

> Disease is the result of breaking Universal Laws. To my mind, the one which is continuously misused is the law that says, 'What we sow we reap, measure for measure'. Or we suffer from wrong thinking being inflicted on us as a child or from our own wrong thinking and sometimes carry a grudge or bitterness in our inner self for many years, until finally it is worked out in the body or the mind . . . I unravel, through clairvoyant diagnosis the person's anxieties, bring them out and solve them and the person begins to get well quite rapidly. (Joan

Bajzert, Surrey, a mental healer)

The linking with cosmic healing forces increases the patient's own self-repair processes. (Mrs Lorna Horstmann, Bath)

The divine source of all life is responsible. The healer acts as a transformer for spiritual forces. These forces must be associated with wavelengths of some type and in some way be electrical in form. (John R Lockwood, Yorkshire)

Question 7 asked, 'What is your own mental and/or spiritual attitude while healing? Do you pray? Meditate? Invoke God? Visualise?' The replies showed a fascinating unanimity despite differing phraseology. Practically everyone said they began with prayer – to God, Eternal Spirit, the Christ Power, Universal Mind – in a spirit of surrender, thanksgiving, love, of asking for help for the patient or to be used as an instrument of healing. Then in reaching a state of attunement they stressed the importance of clearing the mind. The following expressions were typical:

> 'I visualise scenes of nature.'
> 'I try to think of peaceful scenes like a cornfield or slow-moving stream.'
> 'I try to become a complete blank.'
> 'I clear my mind of everyday things and relax.'
> 'I start with mental linking up and request, then keep empty.'
> 'I become as passive as possible.'
> 'Necessary to let go efforts to get results.'
> 'I abandon all activity of the conscious mind and am soon completely still and composed like the surface of a quiet lake.'
> 'I meditate on trees and flowers.'

'This is my point of attunement with Spirit', wrote Victor Harold Child. 'In a further minute or so I receive a strong contraction in the solar plexus region. I then welcome my guides, of which I am aware and have seen several times in visions, and proceed with the individual healing requests. I frequently visualise the patient as already healed.'

'I wait until I see a bright spot of amethyst a distance away. It comes closer and larger until it covers me and then does it over and over again, perhaps six or seven times. When this ceases I know I am ready to treat the patient', said Mrs E A Cooper, who lives on one of the Channel Isles.

'In complete attunement and realising I am only an instrument for spirit use, I simply ask that the right corrective force be transmitted to the patient to overcome their given malady without any doubt in my mind that this will be done', said a healer who did not want his name mentioned.

'I look for a ball or cloud of light inside my head in the forehead region', said Robert Ison, of Cambridge.

Michael Charalambides, of London, wrote:

> I visualise the organ concerned and direct the magnetic current towards it . . . Most of the time I commence with magnetic and finish with spiritual healing. I feel as if I am half asleep, my hands feel numb and heavy and I sense as if someone takes over . . . my hands move unconsciously to other parts of the body in need of diagnosis and healing. Sometimes, with magnetic healing, I feel the urge to command organs to function properly and to my surprise they respond favourably.

Question 35 asked if the healers used clairvoyance, clairaudience or other psychic abilities in healing. A surprising seventy-two per cent said, 'Yes'. Here are some of their added comments:

> 'Clairvoyance allows me to check the patient's state of mind.'
> 'I can see symptoms and reactions.'
> 'I use clairvoyance only when I feel a message can help.'
> 'I was given a message to use clairvoyance only for healing.'

Nearly everybody had a theory on why some do not respond to healing. The patient might be 'too old, too feeble for his recuperative forces to be stimulated adequately.' Or he might be 'surrounded by family who put more faith in the doctor's "no hope" verdict, thus rendering the channel ineffective if loved ones are negative or lack a living faith.' Or, the patient may give up treatment too early, or fail to remove spiritual blocks such as pride, selfishness, egotism, resentment or guilt. As one healer put it, 'Hardness of heart shuts the door.'

They suggested that major operations may disrupt natural functions through which the healing power operates or heavy drugs might inhibit the flow of the healing energy. 'Just as some medicines suit one patient and not another, so there are healers who appear to be successful with some patients and not with others', says Major McDermott, pointing out that even Harry Edwards refers eye patients to his associate, Olive Burton.

Or it might be that patients are not healed because they do not obey simple instructions for improving health habits such as proper sleep and diet or because they give up hope if healing is not immediate. In many cases the ill person may cling to his or her disability to get sympathy and love. 'Closed state of mind, bigots, selfish people, create a barrier within themselves', said one.

'A patient with arthritis may return to a cold, damp home. Then healing is of very little use', said Mrs L G Sharp, of Duston, Northampton.

'Karmic debts, I believe, play a large part', said Marilyn Preston, expressing the view of many. 'A particular lesson may have to be learned, and if the patient gets well before it is learned, that episode will have to be repeated at a later stage.'

"One must be a "fighter" and willing to carry on fighting for his or her own health', said R H Nelson. 'Maybe due to the patient having a negative attitude towards life in general', said Lovell S E Ellis, of Gerrard's Cross, Buckinghamshire. 'For those who are helped, all the conditions are coinciding correctly – the power, the channel, and the patient. When the patient is not helped, the coincidence is not complete or is incorrect', theorises George Sparks.

Reverend Moston was one of the few who thought an apparent healing failure might be due to shortcomings of the healer. 'Like the disciples of old, we are still learning', he wrote. 'The failure may be on our side.'

Their estimates of the numbers of patients healed permanently may have reflected wide differences in experience or the kind of illness in which they specialise. Edwards, for example, who specialises in chronic ailments of the elderly, such as arthritis, said his full cures were thirty per cent of the total. The average estimate of the sample was fifty per cent and the range was from ten per cent to ninety-five per cent. On the other hand, Edwards said eighty per cent report 'betterment', a figure that was concurred in by seventy per cent of the healers. The average estimate was, however, fifty-seven per cent in the 'feel improved' category. (One healer lowered the average by saying only twenty per cent of his patients seemed to benefit.) Only fifty-six per cent ventured an estimate of the numbers of their patients who showed no response at all, and the average of these failures came to nine point eight per cent. 'Each of these had only one session and would not come back', explained one healer. 'These expected instant miracles and did not give healing a chance', said another.

Only thirty-six per cent of the healers would give an estimate of patients who responded instantly in one session. Their estimates averaged twenty-four per cent. They noted the patients suffering from spinal problems, nervous break-downs, headaches and toothaches, although one claimed to have given sight to a blind baby in this manner. Interestingly enough, ninety per cent declared that absent or distant healing is as effective as contact healing, fifteen per cent saying it was 'sometimes better'.

My question looking into the healers' religious back-grounds brought out a variety that, to me, was surprising. By far the greatest number wrote 'Church of England' (or 'C. of E.'), while adding such comments as the following: 'and Spiritualist philosophy'; 'and interested in Spiritualism'; 'but see good in most religions'; 'but got very disillusioned with its dogma'; 'and studied many other religions'; 'as schoolboy, then fifteen years of no interest and then occult subjects, I hope in a balanced way'. This category numbers forty per cent of the sample.

Then came the group who said their background was 'C. of

E. turned Spiritualist' or to 'Christian free-thinker'. They numbered twenty-eight per cent.

Those who gave their background only as Spriritualist was twelve per cent. Many, however, expressed inclination toward other philosophies too, such as metaphysical and esoteric teachings, and an interest in 'all religions'.

Those with Methodist backgrounds numbered ten per cent and included a lay preacher and several who had turned to Spiritualism. 'Turned Spiritualist but can worship in any church or religion in harmony', wrote Walter Roger Smith, and R S Paling said, 'I am now a Spiritualist minister'. There were also Presbyterians (three per cent), half of whom had switched to something else. 'Presbyterian since early youth', wrote Charles MacIntyre of Argyll, Scotland. 'Still a member of the Church of Scotland but, oh dear, I sit in church and feel I could tell the minister a thing or two about the world of Spirit'. Congregationalists were also three per cent, Baptists two per cent (one had turned Spiritualist) and Catholics were eight per cent of the sample. Several, however, had left the church. 'Now Christian Spiritualist, many things have been explained to me'; 'Then Spiritualism, then mysticism'; 'Turned Spiritualist – most reservations'; were a few comments.

Jewish healers numbered four per cent. David Hadda noted 'though not in an institutional sense' while Ivan Arnold Kayes added the word 'Liberal'.

Rounding out the sample were those indicating they were: Christian or Protestant; Christian Orthodox (Greek); or believers in such concepts as 'The Christ', 'The Universal Church', 'A Christian belief in brotherly love and a right way of living'. One of these traced his spiritual search from 'C. of E. to Spiritualists to Quakers and the Society of the Inner Light'.

Judging from the chilly attitude towards spiritual healing of the British Medical Association, the number of healers reporting that patients were referred to them by doctors seemed to me very significant and hopeful. Not all answered the question and some said they had no way of knowing for sure. But nineteen per cent said, 'Yes. I take those the doctors have given up'; 'One doctor asked us for help for his child'; 'Many are advised by their doctors to try spiritual healing';

'Not directly, to my knowledge. But if "by hints", quite often'; were added comments.

A slightly higher percentage – twenty-two per cent – said doctors actually come to them as patients: 'Yes, but I cannot divulge names', 'Once, under strictest confidence'; 'no names mentioned', were remarks added. 'I have cured one of cancer and another of arthritis. Both were German', wrote one healer. 'Have had many people and families from the medical profession – surgeons, sisters, nurses, radiologists', wrote George Sparks. 'I know doctors have had development circles trying to get spirit doctors . . .' said another. Several chimed in with the healer who exclaimed: 'Not yet, but we always hope!'

American healers please note that not one of my respondents charges a fee for healing. Furthermore, it is against the policy of the NFSH. There was an even forty-to-forty split, however, in the numbers saying they accepted donations, the remaining twenty per cent explaining that any donations they accepted were for car fare or stamps or were put in the collection box for their church. Many were vehement, saying, 'Not even for petrol', and 'a divine gift cannot be commercialised'. Others said, 'If they can afford it I do not mind' or 'when offered'.

An important finding, I feel, was the large number (ninety per cent) saying they could help a patient die without pain in cases where a painful passing was expected by doctors. Several mentioned specifically helping advanced cancer patients 'pass over peacefully'. One noted that he had seen 'peace on a troubled face as they passed over and a vision of brightness on both sides of the bed'.

The next step in England's spiritual healing movement, it seems clear, is greater cooperation between individual doctors and spiritual healers leading, hopefully, to full recognition of spiritual healing as a valid alternative therapy by the British Medical Association.

In my personal interviews with widely known healers such as Harry Edwards, Gordon Turner, Ronald Beesley, Mary Rogers, Thomas Johanson, Gilbert Anderson and others, all said many doctors come to them for treatment, although usually quietly without advertising it to their colleagues. And all said they had patients referred to them fairly often by specialists and other doctors who regularly send them baffling or 'hopeless' cases. Combining their testimony with that of the healers answering my questionnaire, it appears that many doctors are defying the BMA's official pronouncement against spiritual healing and that it is only a matter of time before its veto is eroded by the mounting evidence of spiritual healing's effectiveness.

A hopeful step now being taken is the NFSH's own research project to seek evidence that the causes of cancer may be psychosomatic and consequently that the disease is amenable to spiritual healing. Turned down by the British Cancer Council when they proposed a tandem effort, the Federation appointed a distinguished committee headed by Air Marshal Sir Victor Goddard to finance the printing and sending out of questionnaires to cancer patients.

In the offing – perhaps still many years away – is the realisation by the Church of England that spiritual healing belongs in the church, even if it means changing its long-held dogma to concede that the divine healing power may possibly, in some cases, be transmitted through agencies other than Christ and the Holy Spirit.

12

A NEW DOOR OPENS

With the stalemate situation we had reached with regard to our research for cancer patients, I was getting a bit frustrated at the enforced inactivity, yet more and more convinced that the inability to release emotional stress played a very important part in the creation of illness. Going through the post on my desk one morning, I picked up a small magazine and, thumbing through it, a page caught my eye, and I went back to it. The heading of the article was 'The role of the mind in cancer'. Here in print were the almost identical words that had been going through my mind for the past few months. It was written by an American doctor who had cured himself of cancer, and had opened a clinic with his wife, for cancer sufferers.

His theory was very much like my own thoughts, and he was doing most of the things I would like to do, but, as yet, the opportunities would not manifest. He was a radiologist, and his wife a psychotherapist, and they used a form of group therapy. I was so impressed with his approach that I wrote to him, sending a copy of our questionnaire, and other literature we had compiled, suggesting perhaps we might share any of our findings, and so eliminate possible duplication of research. Weeks went by, then months, without a word from him, and my reaction was that because he was a medical man and I was not, he was not interested.

Marcus McCausland was chairman of our research committee, and he referred a doctor to me for possible help. She had cancer, and was due for surgery within a few days. I gave her healing, and said that I had a theory that without knowing it herself she had brought the illness upon herself.

She had been bottling up some deep emotion for a long time and it had finally manifested in disease. She looked at me for a while, then nodded. She revealed that she hated her mother because as far back as she could remember, she had criticised everything she had done. She had resented this for a long time, but it had now turned into a positive hate. This was strange, because this doctor was a brilliant medical scientist, and very successful in her profession and, as far as I could judge, a sensible, clear thinking person.

I asked her if she would try an experiment with me, which I believed might work. She agreed, so I pointed out that the only person being affected by the feelings of hate was the doctor herself – not her mother. I asked her to try and send her mother love, instead of hate – and if that was impossible, at least feel sorry for her, because there was obviously something eating away inside her to make her act as she did. We talked the situation over for a long time. Her mother lived in Switzerland, and she in London. Every year she visited her mother as a duty, but these visits never lasted for more than a day, or two, at most, when the doctor would pack her bags, and come home again, and this had been the pattern for years. I asked her at the end of our session whether she thought my idea made sense. She replied that it did and that she was going to try very hard to carry it through. Before she came to see me she was terrified at the thought of surgery, but now she felt quite different and was sure everything would be all right.

She had the operation and, after coming round from the anaesthetic, the consultant said he had done the best he could but had not been able to remove all the tumour and that she would need intensive radiotherapy to try and destroy what was left. However, she declined to have the radiotherapy saying that she had found something else which she thought could help her far more than radiotherapy. We worked out this new therapy together, and six months' later the cancer had completely gone. That was in 1973 and she said that it was too valuable to keep to ourselves, and that we must share it with other people. Then again, God working in mysterious ways, opened another door. A letter came from the American doctor who I thought had passed me by. He had used some of our ideas, and he and his wife were coming to London and he wanted to meet and discuss things further.

We did meet, and had a most productive day discussing our respective approaches. He had found our questionnaire very helpful, using it for the in-depth examination of the patients to find the initial causes of their problems, and was eager to use the biofeedback machine that Ann Woolley-Hart, my colleague, had used in her researching, and we were using to monitor depth of meditation. He explained his approach which was, as I had done with Ann, to trace back and find the suppressed emotional problems, talk them through, so that the patient had a good idea of the reason for their present ill health then, together with the radiotherapy which he used, he would gather a number of patients together for group therapy. I had never been an advocate for group therapy, believing that if a person had a deep problem that they regretted, they would not discuss it openly in front of other people. But this was rather different. He still had his one-to-one relationship for the very important in-depth counselling, after which they all had a similar problem to face, they all had cancer, and the idea now was to do something positive to improve the quality of their lives. As a group they were encouraged to talk openly about their disease and, without realising it, they helped each other in this way. His success rate was quite high, and gave us the resolve to start without further delay. As Administrator, I had access to hundreds of patients' records, from which I could pick out some very advanced terminal cases, and see if we could help to improve the quality of what life they had left, on the principle that we are all going to die (that is the one thing we can be certain of), but we do not know when. So, instead of spending what time we have left worrying about dying, let us think about living, and make the best of what we have got, so long as it is here.

I selected seven patients whose medical life expectancy ranged from one week to three months, and asked them if they were prepared to help us with an experiment. We could not promise that it would be any help, but it would not make them any worse. We told them what we wanted to do, and they all gladly agreed to come into it. We then took them back individually through their lives, bringing to the surface any emotion that they had been unable to resolve, talked it through, until they realised that nothing of any help to anyone had resulted from the suppression of the problem but, they themselves, had suffered sickness as a result.

Our individual therapy went along the following lines. It is pointless living in the past nurturing hates, fears, resentments, rejection, feelings of inadequacy, or any other negative feelings about things that have happened in the past. They have happened, and nothing can be done to change it, so accept it, whatever it was, learn from it if you can, then let it go. All of these experiences, good or bad, are part of life, and one can usually gain something useful from them. If, for instance, you have done something that you are ashamed of, provided you do not continue making the same mistake again, you have learned a useful lesson. One can usually look back after the event, and be thankful for the experience. But, not satisfied with this waste of time, and energy, regretting the past, serious illness prompts one to look forward, also with anxiety and fear, but this again is anticipation. We cannot be sure until it actually happens.

If we cannot change the past, or control the future, what are we left with? The one crucial fact – NOW. We are living now, this moment of this day, and we have control of each moment throughout this day. Just a few hours to do something useful with. Make up your mind that you will make these few hours as enjoyable, and useful, as you can, so that when you start your next today you are starting it with a plus not a minus. No wasted time, and energy, on useless negativity, but a positive step forward to do something useful.

What other aids are at our disposal? – breathing. How often does one think seriously about something that we have done naturally from birth? Stop this one fundamental activity, however, and your physical life is at an end. Our body is a wonderfully constructed mechanism, with a marvellous governing control. It has its own inbuilt maintenance system which will keep it healthy until we interfere with its natural healthy function either by physical, mental or emotional misuse. The body signals us when problems are developing, but how often do we heed them until too late? Two of the finest aids to overcome weakness, or sickness, are purposeful breathing and a positive attitude. Simple things, natural things, but things that we give little, or no, serious thought to.

How does one get away from the bad habits of a lifetime?

Calming the mind through regular meditation, where thoughts can be directed away from the everyday problems of life, towards pleasant relaxing and enjoyable scenes that will bring a measure of peace. In the quiet of the mind one can see problems in their true perspective, not distorted and magnified, as worry so often creates. Now one becomes aware of a control over thought, emotions and bodily functions, often for the first time. Another vital factor is the knowledge that our body is changing throughout the whole of our life. Cells are being discarded, and reproduced, every moment of our life, and we can help this process with our thoughts and breathing.

Our group therapy was based on the knowledge that the average cancer patient spends most of their time at home, are often treated by friends and acquaintances as though they have some contagious disease, simply because people do not know what to say to them, and they will avoid them, if possible, to save embarrassment. There has been so much fear built round the word 'cancer' that people are afraid to voice it, with the result that a cancer patient tends to be isolated when they need help most. So, wherever possible, we would encourage the partner, or a close member of the family, in our group work, so that they can give the patient all possible support by taking part in it, both in the group, and at home. We decided our group would meet once every two weeks, on the understanding that its members would make a regular daily practice of what we taught them in the group, at home.

We impressed upon them that this was their problem, and we were not solving it for them. We would show them what to do, and how to do it, giving them all the help and support necessary for them to start helping themselves, reminding them that their life, body, thoughts and emotions were all theirs, and they should take more responsibility for them.

Our group consisted of five patients (two had died before we had time to start the therapy) and their partners, who sat in a semicircle in front of us, each patient linked to a relaxometer. These meters worked on skin conductivity registering brain impulses through the sweat glands of the hands. The electrodes were attached to the finger tips, and indicated, very accurately, the degree to which we were able to 'talk them down' into a state of calm relaxation. We found them invaluable, because it is impossible to tell to what depth of meditation one has reached by just looking at the patient with their eyes closed.

The general procedure was that we would ask them what their experiences had been prior to the meeting, any medical reports, tests, how they had felt etc. then, prior to starting the relaxation, some deep breathing, and stretching, to become very aware of the difference between tension and relaxation. We would then talk them down into a state of physical and mental relaxation with meditation on pleasant scenes, watching their individual meters to see their reaction. Having got their minds quiet and relaxed, we then suggested they look inside their body – how do you see the disease? Try and get an image in your mind of how you see it, and whatever you see, set about trying to clear it away – let your imagination take over. No matter how silly a picture you may have, the important thing to remember is – use your own body building mechanism to help clear away any unwanted intrusions, by breathing out disease, and breathing in the cosmic life force, and see your body beginning to respond. Ann was an inspiration to them. She would say – look, if I can do it, so can you, come on, it is early days yet. She was a tower of strength to me too. I had watched her change from a very down to earth medical researcher, into a deep thinking spiritual lady able to give just the right measure of advice at the appropriate time, to keep them going in the right direction.

After two months the patients started coming in with reports from their GPs. The consultants could not understand that the patients were better than on their previous visits.

And so weeks went by, and still they were not only still with us, but had transformed from a rather sorry group of sick people into a happy, laughing group, who were a joy to be with. We started the group in May. By August not one of them should have survived but, here they were, asking if we could close the group for a few weeks because they wanted to go on holiday. It was six weeks before we met together again. Going through the usual procedures of asking how they had enjoyed their holidays, we asked if they had continued with their daily meditation. Most had attempted to maintain their meditation, but some had found they were too busy while entertaining guests, or while on rock-climbing holidays! So much for their death sentences.

After six months one of the doctors on our research team – he was the Senior Consultant Physician for the Plymouth Group of Hospitals – came to see what was going on. He saw and talked to the patients, examined their records and said, 'I do not believe it, these people should all have died from their medical records but, not only are they still alive, they are really living. If this is what can be done, I am into it.' He was Dr Alec Forbes, and he gave up his medical practice, and opened the original Bristol Cancer Help Centre. By the end of the first year we had five healthy patients enjoying a much fuller life than they had ever done before. Harry Edwards was all for advertising this success, but we preferred to give it a few more months first, because we had yet to receive confirmation from the hospital consultants that they were clear. This was the first time I had disagreed with Harry Edwards, but we stuck to our decision not to publish the result. So he decided to use the results of this pilot study, and launch his own cancer therapy with absent healing from his sanctuary at Shere.

So, why did we get involved in this form of therapy, and what brought it about initially? The rest of this chapter is devoted to a paper we wrote on a natural approach to dealing with cancer.

A natural approach to dealing with cancer

After many years of studying health, sickness and our way of life, we are more than ever convinced that now is the time for a serious reassessment of our behavioural habits if we are to stand any chance of combating the ever-increasing stresses of modern living. The tempo of life increases year by year, everything is speeding up, noise is on the increase, environmental pollution of air, water and food is building up, cost of living spiralling ever upwards, adding to the many stresses and anxieties from other aspects of our lives. With all these growing problems is it any wonder that so many forms of illness and disease are on the increase?

It is becoming an accepted fact that the majority of disease and sickness has its origin in the emotional make-up of the individual. Two people subjected to the same stresses and emotional problems will seldom react the same. Some are introvert, often unable to express emotions openly and easily, keeping them bottled up, while others are extrovert and very easy outgoing. It is this difference in our make-up that creates this individuality, so that every person needs to be looked at, treated and understood for what they are. The recognised mass grouping of people having a specific complaint and receiving the same treatment just does not work.

With our present health system and the overwork and thoughtless abuse of the doctor by many people, we must think seriously about a little self help. If, as we believe, most of our ill health is self-induced due to our inability to throw off our emotional problems, allowing them to both multiply and magnify, then we should first look to ourselves trying to see what has gone wrong. Then we will most likely find the answer.

Who does your body and your life belong to? If the answer is 'me', have you seriously considered any sort of responsibility for keeping it healthy? Would you abuse your motor car as you so often do your physical body without expecting it to break down? Probably not. Yet we treat our body with utter disregard for the wonder of its mechanism, and still complain if it fails to give a hundred per cent performance.

Ponder for a moment on this wonderfully constructed physical mechanism of the body, marvel at its unique function. Think of the brain as the intricate computer that it is, conveying instruction to every part of the body throughout the whole of its earthly life. The construction of the physical body is such that it will serve us faithfully and well for the normal duration of this life provided we do not interfere with its perfect function.

Allowing anxieties free rein, as is often the case, is rather like trying to drive a car without any previous knowledge or instruction – you just do not know what to do with your hands or feet to synchronise them, with the result that they do everything that you do not want them to. This is basically what happens to the body when thoughts get mixed up and confused, the computer is being fed incorrect information, with the result that the body is not getting the answering response wanted. No computer will give a right answer unless the correct information is fed in initially. So long as positive thought instruction is fed through the brain, the body will respond and behave healthily, allowing the natural energy to flow unobstructed through the circulatory, glandular and nervous systems, ensuring correct cell production and maintaining the body's immune system in perfect working order. This means then that the two most important factors in our life to either maintain or regain good health are thoughts and correct purposeful breathing. We exist in a constant sea of cosmic energy (life force). This is our only means of physical life, yet we give little thought to the importance of our breathing and what it really means to us.

If you will think positively and breathe purposefully you can actually feel the new energy and vitality building up within you. On the reverse side, if we allow a continual flow of anxieties, hates, resentments, fears, feelings of guilt and other negative emotions to occupy our thoughts, the brain is passing this muddled negative instruction through to the body, creating disharmony and obstruction to the vital energy flow. If this situation is allowed to continue unrestricted, the chances are that some form of illness will result. Starving the body of its vital fuel and careless breathing impose strains on the body that it is not capable of coping with because it has been robbed of the necessary strength to carry out the duties for which it is equipped. This brings us back to the vital question again: whose responsibility is your health?

If we stop to think, there is so much we can do to improve ourselves and our health by accepting more self-responsibility. Give the poor doctor a chance to get his or her second wind. We can often do more and better for ourselves than he or she can. We are not just the physical beings that so many of us have developed into through our own material involvement. We are threefold beings – body, mind and spirit – but the mind has lost its way in so many instances and wanders aimlessly into such dense undergrowth of materialism that it becomes lost and confused and unable to orientate its right direction.

The spirit too has become so suppressed over the years of adult life that in many cases its existence is completely forgotten, Yet it is this spiritual part of us that is the real immortal us. Within each one of us is that divine spark which gave us our being, linking us with all other forms of life and the source of all creation. This inner self is a vital source of peaceful, calming energy, always there for us to draw on, yet so many have isolated themselves from it by a hard crust of materialism.

So, how can we find it, and improve our whole outlook and reaction to life? If it is not possible to change our environment, we must find a way of protecting ourselves against its destructive influence. Our need is freedom from anxiety and emotional upsets through a peaceful, tranquil mind.

We have talked about breathing as a source of energy. We can also utilise it in a purposeful way to help rid ourselves of unwanted negative thoughts and anxieties as well as physical pain and sickness. Breathe out fully, clearing lungs and stomach, with the thought in your mind that you are ridding yourself of all disharmony both of mind and body – then breathe in slowly but fully with the knowledge that you are breathing in the cosmic life force that will help to create and establish a feeling of peace and determination to accept life and its problems as a challenge that we should face up to and try to understand. Not necessarily fight, because as we begin to understand our problems we see that we have magnified and distorted them out of all recognition. Now, seeing them as they really are, it becomes so much easier to deal with them.

Having established the purpose of this form of breathing in your consciousness, reduce the depth of breathing a little concentrating your attention on the easy rhythmic feel of your breathing out (to a count of three) and in (to a count of three). (As correct purposeful breathing is most important for the realisation of this inner peace and greater self-dependence and thought control, it is dealt with more fully later in this chapter under the heading of 'Relaxation, meditation and seeing within oneself for positive thought directive'.)

To show how one's changed attitude can completely reverse a serious health condition, the following pilot study was undertaken, which has proved to be most encouraging. Although this study was confined to a specific disease, I am convinced that the same approach can be applied to most other forms of illness or disease.

From previous research it seemed fairly certain that stress in many and varied forms was largely responsible for much of the disease in the world today – particularly that of suppressed emotion for which there is no outlet. If this is so, and the situation could be changed by removing or releasing these stress factors and creating within the individual the will to live and something to fight for, it seemed possible that a reversal of the situation might well result.

Both Drs Simonton, Woolley-Hart and myself have been cancer sufferers and we feel sure that we have been helped to overcome this disease by other agencies in addition to medical science – either by spiritual healing, a changed attitude and determination to live – or a combination of both. With spiritual healing we are dealing with some form of energy which to date has defied scientific measurement on any form of instrument. There are magnetic energy fields around the body, but these are not responsible for bringing about the exceptional chemical/physical changes which are manifest through this spiritual source – often in the space of a few minutes. Such changes come within the total laws of nature but not necessarily on a known physical level. Medical science, concerned as it is with the physical body, cannot always meet the full need of the patient. There is also a spiritual need. Healing should be holistic, treating the spiritual as well as the physical being, and it is the combining of these two pathways that should concern us for the overall well-being of the patient. There can be little doubt that many forms of energy yet remain to be uncovered by man, and research into the psychic and spiritual levels of existence has disclosed much evidence of this. The fact of a tumour dispersing under the hands of a healer, calcified joints being restored to normal mobility, misplaced discs replaced without physical manipulation on the part of the healer, all point to the existence of both powers and intelligence superior to our present understanding. Doctors who have witnessed such healings are agreed that they cannot be explained by orthodox medical theory. The growing acceptance of this non-physical approach is indicated by the fact that since 1958 healers have been admitted into 1,500 national hospitals to cooperate in the healing of the sick.

The question of 'healing' is not one that should surprise people for it is several thousand years old. It is far more reasonable to question our own concepts of consciousness and energy. Despite the remarkable advances made in 'neurophysiology' we are still no nearer to understanding the nature of consciousness and what actually initiates the impulses in the brain (although the neural pathways exist for receiving and transmitting information). It appears as if consciousness interacts with our cerebral mechanisms and directs them: we are souls inhabiting physical bodies.

As stated earlier in the chapter, in the beginning we invited seven very advanced terminal patients with varying forms of cancer which included leukaemia, bone cancer, breast cancer, lung cancer and uterine malignancy, to take part in this first pilot study. Two of these died before it was possible to start the therapy. In June 1974 after a thorough investigation into their past histories to search out their hidden stresses and release them, we commenced our group therapy with the five terminal patients. First, it was necessary to eliminate the fear that their terminal verdict had created, and to put in its place a spark of hope. We believed the patients themselves had in many instances brought the disease into being by negative attitudes due to stress, such as the suppression of fear, hate, envy, resentment, or other forms of worry that had taken control of their thoughts. Therefore, by reversing the mental process it should then be possible to bring the body back to a more normal state of health.

Generally speaking, we become so engrossed in the material way of life, with its ever-increasing struggle for earthly gain and survival, that we lose sight of the most valuable asset life has bestowed upon us. This is the appreciation that we are not wholly physical beings but that we have a spiritual part of our life as well. It is in this area of experience that we can find peace of mind and an understanding of life's fuller purpose.

The physical body is controlled by the brain – our body's computer and to whose impulses our body responds. Like any other computer, if fed with the wrong information it cannot give the correct answer. It would seem logical, therefore, that if one thinks negatively, the body's natural healthy function will begin to break down and conversely, by thinking positively, the body is helped to restore its normal control of function. This will include immunity.

The purpose of the group therapy was to teach relaxation and meditation so making people more receptive to spiritual healing which is given during their relaxation by the laying on of hands. The most difficult part of the procedure was to eliminate the constant flow of negative thoughts that impinge so insistently on consciousness and destroy peace of mind. In their place, positive constructive thoughts on health and well being are considered.

It was not long, however, before an encouraging reaction began to show itself within the group. The morose gathering of people who had started the study began to show more and more evidence of a happier state of mind. Smiling faces and laughter became a prominent factor as soon as they met together in animated discussion as to who had made the most progress over the past week or two – thus introducing between them a friendly but competitive spirit. As month followed month the medical reports also became more encouraging: 'My drugs have been reduced'; 'The consultant cannot understand the change, it is quite contrary to the normal pattern'; 'I am so thrilled, my blood is normal'; 'The last X-ray shows the shadow much less and I feel fine'; 'I have been able to do some gardening without any ill effect and the specialist said I would never be able to do anything like that again.'

So crucial work has pressed on and, from time to time, new patients were introduced into the group. After two years, three of those terminal patients survived, in whom medical examination indicated no trace of cancer. Of the two deaths – one patient suffered from the side effects of radiation treatment and another succumbed to severe shock when the specialist whom she idolised was killed in a bomb incident.

With this encouraging response to the pilot study, other groups were being set up in various parts of the country. The following gives some idea of our approach to the disease. The patients are taught correct breathing and relaxation. They are then asked to use positive thinking and mental imagery to see the disease in their own bodies and how they can envisage the body's defence mechanism overcoming it. During the relaxation it was thought that people might be more receptive to the healing they were to be given. The technique also helps to create a personal sense of responsibility for health and well being.

What is cancer?

This is a condition where groups of cells in an organ start to grow and form colonies on their own. The mechanisms of control that normally prevent this have been lost and so the cell colonies grow very big until they destroy much of the organ. Sometimes small pieces break off and get carried to other parts of the body or the cells grow outside the original organ and spread locally, causing destruction and even obstruction of neighbouring organs and tissues. Normally there are cells in the body whose function it is to seek out foreign material and remove it. These cells act like a police force to keep law and order and they recognise foreign invaders. Such cells are: white blood cells; antibodies; phagocytes; reticulo-endrothelial cells and many others. They form part of our immunity system and provide a means of recognising 'self from not-self' – this last including our own cells in places where they have no business to be.

Now in disease – especially in cancer – this police force is not working properly and we ought to consider why. Firstly, there may be something different about the cancer cell – perhaps they have a kind of camouflage? While there are many reasons for believing this to be so, it is of greater importance to ask what has gone wrong with us to allow this to happen.

About stress and emotional problems.

During the first few years of our lives our patterns of behaviour tend to get set. Very soon in a baby's life there comes a time when it tries to get its own way and meets with opposition. The parents become cross and scold the baby and a very natural reaction is that the baby fears loss of its parents' love. If this occurs often it may give rise to a sense of rejection in the child, but since love and security are what every young child craves, certain defence mechanisms arise. These are as if the child said:

1. If you love me you will do what I say.
2. If I am very good and do what you want, you will not hurt me.
3. If I cannot be seen then you will not know I am there and cannot hurt me.
4. I do not care so I will do what I like anyway.

These childhood reactions tend to get carried over into adult life. We may have long forgotten what caused them, but our later attitudes are often subconsciously coloured by one or more of these early patterns. And because of these patterns, we may not see life-situations clearly but from our own biased viewpoint. This in turn may give rise to feelings of anger, resentment, insecurity, rebellion, rejection, or lead to unresolved conflicts and guilt. Such reactions prevent us from being 'ourselves'. They lead to images of ourselves as we think we ought to be, rather than what we really are. In addition, the environment in our home, school, period of training for work etc., condition us to play particular roles, for example: the child, the pupil, the parent, the friend, the worker. How often had one heard or said 'he (or she) is quite different at work, or away from home?' These differing aspects of ourselves, intensified by emotional undercurrents, can become warring factions. These, of course, are present in everyone's life, but some of us can integrate and come to terms with them better than others. Those of us unable to do so, tend to become ruled by the inner conflict we cannot see, and lose our ability to direct our lives. One way round this is to sit back calmly and ask oneself 'who' one is, to try and observe which role one is playing and to consider if it is the best one for the situation. In that way one becomes the observer of oneself and one's behaviour and so can take control, and become more integrated. If we do not do this, our conflicts create a form of stress that affects the way our bodies function. Conflicts are just as much a stress for our system as is overwork, a serious car accident or physical danger. In most cases they are more insidious because they are long-term in action, have no exterior tangibility and as time passes can erode away the body's reserves.

The body reacts to stress of any sort in a simple way. It prepares us today as in our primitive times, for survival by 'fight' or 'flight'. Now we cannot go around punching everyone on the jaw who threatens or annoys, neither can we run away every time people or life frightens us. So we come to live under a permanent state of tension that never has a proper outlet. The body reacts to these stresses by altering the blood flow for our skin and internal organs in favour of the muscles, heart or brain, preparing us for a big physical effort that never comes. In addition, some of our glands become very active. Much thyroid hormone is secreted as well as adrenalin and cortisone. So we feel anxious and worried or we become aggressive to cover up our insecurity. At this point we can understand how stress affects our body's police force. It is very well known in medicine that cortisone destroys our immune reactions, and in stress we have a raised output of cortisone.

The cancer personality.

So far we have talked about stress, emotional problems in the early years and our way of reacting. Obviously, what has been said is a large over-simplification and not the only cause of illness. It doubtless only touches the surface of the problem. It just serves to outline the kind of events that lead to stress. Stress makes us anxious and anxiety is a killer. Of course, it is not always cancer that results but, when it does, there seem to be certain personality-factors that create a cancer 'pattern'. What we have to ask ourselves is – how much of the following picture fits us:

1. Have we got a negative attitude towards life and people?
2. Have we got a poor image of ourselves?
3. Are we the anxious, worrying type, with persistent unresolved problems?
4. Do we have the 'will to live' or are we using our disease as an escape?

5. Have we got a poor emotional relationship with others?
6. Do we believe we have been rejected in some manner in life, especially in childhood?

An affirmative response to these questions shows the kind of person who might get cancer. Actually, it seems very likely that nearly everyone of us has cancer cells in our body, at one time or another. Often such events in our lives as a recent bereavement, a severe accident or an extra bout of 'stress' can lead to these independent cells flourishing – but normally, our natural defence mechanisms go to work to 'throw them off'.

What can we do about our cancer?

A young radiotherapy doctor in America has been using relaxation-meditation techniques very effectively. In them one must relax both physically and mentally as deeply as one can. These techniques can be taught. In the relaxed state it is necessary to form a picture of the cancer process inside oneself, to envisage a picture of the disease as it appears to us, and to relate it to our bodies – then to try and see how the body relates to it. Finally, one should think of the treatment one is having – whether orthodox or from a healer. Try to see how it is helping destroy the disease and imagine how the immune responses of the body fit in with the help one is receiving from outside. Then envisage the mobilisation of the body's defence mechanism as it fights to overcome the invader. One should try to get a mental picture of the whole process. Also the picture must have meaning and one must be able to relate to it with feeling.

It has been said what we *think* we *become,* and it must be remembered that thought is a form of energy. Therefore, if we imagine ourselves well and have the genuine wish to become well, we stand the chance of being well. Perhaps you ask, 'Why relax for all this?' The reason is this: we have already said that our nervous system under arousal reacts in a certain manner which is a preparation for battle. If we really relax, it is exactly this reaction which is *prevented* from taking place.

At this point then our nervous systems have the chance of regaining the lost, but proper balance. Also, when we are relaxed and contemplate upon our problems, they often lose their emotional content. We see a way to cope with them and we gain insights about ourselves and our responsibilities. This is being the 'observer'. Sometimes the truth is unpleasant and frightening but we must not allow ourselves to become depressed. After all, behind the mask everyone shows to the world, each has problems of one sort or another that require specific means of coping and solving.

We are not claiming that relaxation and meditation is easy. There is no short cut to learning it properly, and it must be practised every day for at least thirty minutes. During relaxation one often begins to see things more clearly. This is only the beginning though because there now comes the fight with ourselves to try to make the necessary changes. It is a daily battle – change does not come quickly. It is most especially difficult with the immediate problems we must meet each day. However, if correctly done, the daily meditation period will lead to an increase in feelings of calmness. This process can be observed very simply by instrumental measurement of the size of a tiny current passed through the palm of the hand. From this, progress can be checked, and it can be seen how well we have learned to relax. The same method will also be used in the relaxation training.

Relaxation, meditation, and seeing within oneself for positive thought direction.

To be able to obtain the inner quiet necessary for the full cooperation response of mind and body towards this mental directive, it is necessary to relax, both mentally and physically. As this is one of the most difficult aspects of the therapy, we hope the following guiding procedure with your relaxation and meditation will be of help.

>   1. Sit in an upright chair with your back straight (this is the correct and natural posture of the body and a position which you can retain for a

long period without feeling any strain) legs uncrossed with feet on the floor and your hands resting, lightly on your knees. Now, to appreciate when you are relaxed – stretch yourself from head to foot, extend your arms as far as you can, now your legs, and your head. Now flop, and feel the difference between tension and relaxation. Repeat this exercise three or four times then sit quietly relaxed.
2. We need to eliminate all external distractions that our eyes might take in, so close your eyes and sit quiet, not thinking of anything in particular, just letting yourself relax.
3. Correct breathing is a most important factor both towards relaxation and mental stimulation (for correct thought directive). First, breathe out fully with the thought in your mind that you are ridding yourself of every negative destructive element within you, both mental and physical, such as: worry, fear, resentments, physical pain or discomfort. Feel that you are consciously ridding yourself of it as you breathe out. Then breathe in slowly and fully, with the thought firmly in your mind that you are breathing in the cosmic energy of life force that creates and maintains all life. Imagine you are having your 'batteries' recharged and feel new life and energy being taken into your body. Then as you again exhale, do it with the knowledge that you are discarding everything in your mind and body that is creating disharmony: breathe it right out and take in fresh life and vitality again. Repeat this a dozen or so times until the full import of the exercise has registered on your consciousness, and while you are doing it try to feel this change taking place, both in your mind and body. Now reduce your depth of breathing to about half of the maximum, so that you are taking in more than you normally do. Breathe in to a count of three, hold for a few seconds then

exhale at the same rate, so that you are getting a steady rhythmic form of breathing which will relax you. To get the rhythm more firmly into your conscious thoughts, visualise in your mind's eye, either a pendulum swinging to this rhythm or yourself standing on a sandy beach at the ebb tide, at the water's edge, watching the gentle ripple to and fro of the wavelets. Continue this form of breathing until you feel completely at peace within.

4. Now disassociate your thoughts from all outside influences and turn them within. Imagine you are looking inside yourself instead of looking outwards and direct your thoughts down through your body to the tips of your toes. Think of your limbs as being absorbent and your thoughts moisture. Mentally command your toes to relax and feel them physically respond. Then let these relaxing thoughts be absorbed slowly and smoothly up through your feet – insteps, heels, ankles and on up through your calves. Feel the muscle response as you go, through your knees, thighs, buttocks, into the back and stomach, coming to rest in the solar plexus. This is the visceral 'brain' of your nervous system, ie. an area where shocks and tensions will register most forcibly. Mentally, smooth away any feeling of unrest or disturbance that may be here. Do not hurry, be sure that you have a feeling of complete peace and calm here, before moving on. Leave that nice peaceful feeling there and take your thoughts to the top of your head, and, as though they are oil, let them pour smoothly down, over your forehead, on down past your cheeks and ears. Feel your jaws slacken and relax, and then continue down your throat and neck; pause at the base of your neck and shoulders (another point of accumulative tension), feel your shoulders slacken and relax. Then move on

through the shoulders down your arms to the finger tips and down your back and chest returning again to the solar plexus.
5. Now, in this more relaxed state, use a similar exercise for cleansing your body by trying to draw off any disease that may be there. This time picture your thoughts as a sponge, and this sponge is going to absorb disease and disharmony into it as you take it slowly through your body. Start again at the toes then take these absorbing thoughts slowly up through the feet and legs. Draw off any disease, disharmony, pain or disability as you go smoothly on up the body, and continue up the arms and chest and right on through the head. Then pretend you have a trap door or window in the top of your head, open it and let all this disharmony go out. Then firmly close it again to ensure it does not return. Now, if you think of the sun's rays as the cosmic energy of life, try and visualise this warm golden ray shining down on top of your head. Let it soak into your body, bringing with it a feeling of comfort and warmth of love that permeates your whole being.
6. You should now be feeling relaxed, with your thoughts concerned with bringing your physical body under their control and both your mind and body should be at peace and divorced from the mundane material worries that beset you. Hold this feeling of peace and really enjoy it.
7. Into your mind create a picture of any condition which you know will give you a feeling of pleasurable peace and tranquillity. This could be a favourite garden, standing by the seashore, walking through a wood, lazing by the banks of a stream or any other condition in which you can find complete relaxation and happy peaceful memories. Stay with this picture and try to become a part of it. Feel the

warmth of the sun on your body, the soft caress of the breeze on your face, the scent of flowers, trees or sea, and listen to the soft murmur of nature and become part of it.

8. In this relaxed condition you are preparing your body to receive and act upon healthy positive thought direction. Your brain is the computer which controls bodily function. By feeding into it the positive, healthy instruction you can help it combat disease. You are in effect helping to produce a strong and powerful force of white blood cells, antibodies, phagocytes and other policing agencies to overcome and destroy the enemy, your disease. By your positive thought control of your body in this way, the correct immunity system will be restored to maintain a healthy bodily function.

9. With this in mind, explore your body from inside and do have a jolly good look round to see where it is not working properly. Take a good hard look at the disease. What does it look like to you? Get a picture of it clearly in your mind. Now, all the time you are building up strength with positive thoughts and purposeful breathing, your combat force of antibodies is growing in strength and determination to restore health and overthrow the enemy. You know this, so *you* are in command of these forces. See how best you can employ them to destroy your enemy. What tactics are you going to employ? This is your personal battle, but remember you have the power of spiritual healing working with you continually under your thought control to master the situation. The only limits to the power of our mind and spiritual healing are those we impose ourselves.

10. Go to work then – with a mind bomb of determination that together we can and will see if we as well as our disease are not

incurable.
11. We do not speak idly when we say you must make this a regular daily minimum half-hour session – this is most important. Experience has shown us the vital need for this if you want to get well. If you have time for more – so much the better.

Medical response after two years of the study.

Top British doctors observed the sessions and confirmed that four patients were doing unbelievably well. 'These patients should all have died within a year,' said Dr Ian Pearce, a general practitioner of thirty years' experience. 'I would not hesitate to recommend one of my patients to Mr Anderson.'

Dr Alec Forbes, a consultant at Plymouth General Hospital and an Oxford trained Fellow of the Royal College of Physicians, has seen the medical records of the four patients. He said, 'The patients in the group are living almost impossibly long beyond the normal course of their disease. Not only are they still alive, but they are leading normal lives and seem to be perfectly healthy.'

Dr John Warren, a chest specialist at St Margaret's Hospital near London who trained at London Hospital, thought his lung cancer patient would never survive. 'I would have said he had only a few months to live', he recalled.

Dr Ralph Twentyman of the Royal Homoeopathic Hospital where some of the Queen's doctors are affiliated, was impressed: 'She's making a good recovery', he conceded referring to his patient Dr Woolley-Hart. 'The treatment she is receiving from Mr Anderson seems to be doing her a lot of good.'

Into this original pilot group four other patients were added at intervals, in 1975 and 1976 and two of these are still living.

Extending these groups.

In 1976 a group was started in the Royal London Homoeopathic Hospital with seven patients, three of whom are still living and two known to be working. In 1976 a group was started in Norfolk with the cooperation of Dr Ian Pearce which is also showing very satisfactory results. In 1977 a group was started in the Nature Cure Clinic in London and of the six patients in that group three are living.

The one outstanding feature with all the patients who have taken part in these groups is the wonderfully improved quality of their lives, whether the extension of the life has been short, or long, the enhanced quality has brought a richness never before experienced. As one has said, 'If I die tomorrow, I will be eternally grateful for four and a half of the most wonderful years that Bill and I have ever known.'

13

MOVING ON FROM THE NFSH

At one of Harry Edwards's monthly visits to us he was discussing our arrangements for the Annual Bazaar with Ruth, and suggested we might have a clairvoyant this time to give readings, and add a little income that way. He knew of a new medium from the north of England – he said she was just starting but was very good, and it would help her too. So we invited her down. Ruth thought she would try her out, and go in incognito and see what she got. The medium accurately described Ruth's three brothers who had all died of cancer, and that her fourth brother was also suffering from cancer. She also said that she visualised changes – keys being handed over.

The following day the chairman called Ruth aside and said he knew her brother was ill and wondered whether she would like to resign so as to devote more time to her brother. He also suggested that I may like to hand over the administration but to continue as research director. The chairman represented a 'new broom', but when he put the proposal to me I was prepared for the break and in actual fact I preferred the research work which was getting quite exciting, so I agreed.

And who was the medium who had been so accurate about handing over keys? She was the very well-known medium, the late Doris Stokes, just starting off on her public career. She had also told Ruth her brother would not see the New Year, and he died on New Year's Eve.

It was not long before the effect of the new broom at the NFSH became obvious, with changes of general policy, and the writing of personal letters to people who were asking for help, which I had always written, and obviously meant a lot to the recipient, stopped. In their place, a brief stereotyped note acknowledging their request, was sent instead. I began getting feedback from people who disagreed with the changing policy, as I did. At the next executive meeting I was asked to take my retirement a year early, as the new administrator found it difficult working with me. This was not surprising because it was a complete change, with money seeming to be the controlling factor.

We stayed on in the coach house for two months until deciding to sell our bungalow at Denton in Norfolk because of our involvement with the Loughton Players Old Tyme Music Hall company and the many friends we had made in Loughton. I was told by the administrator that he was taking over the cancer group and it was no longer our responsibility. I gave this up reluctantly, because it had now been running for two years. After this we moved back to our bungalow in Denton and put it up for sale.

Over a period of three months we had four abortive attempts at selling our bungalow but came to the conclusion that we were not meant to sell it, so took it off the market. Having made that decision we arranged to go back to Loughton, and tell our friends that we would not be returning after all. We took the caravan, and parked it on a site in the town – we had bought the caravan mainly so that we could take our dog, Tara, with us on holidays. We had also arranged to have a sitting with a medium friend at the Greater World headquarters, to see if she, Christine Burnett-Smith, could throw any light on our problems. We arrived there in pouring rain, and she told us to bring our dog indoors because she was not very well – this was news to us to start. She then told us that there would be three prospective purchasers for our bungalow – one would be doubtful but the other two would be serious purchasers. She ended the sitting by saying that we definitely would be moving back to Loughton but that Tara will not be with us.

After this sitting I telephoned my neighbour in Denton and he reported that after we had been gone for only a couple of hours people were almost 'queuing up' to look over it. One couple were just out for a ride, and wanted to look, but not buy. The other two, however, were almost waiting on the doorstep for our return. We agreed to return next day and in the morning when I was hitching up the caravan Ruth said, 'What is the matter with Tara?' I looked, and she was rolled over on her back, with her head dropped on one side. She was obviously ill, so we dashed her off to the vet's. She had had a heart attack, not a severe one, but the vet told us she was eaten up with cancer and she had survived four years longer than she should have done, so we had to expect her to die pretty soon. We got her home safely, and made her comfortable, telephoned the vet in Harleston, and made an appointment for next day. We had not been home an hour when the telephone rang. It was one of the prospective buyers wanting to come over. We made the appointment, and they duly arrived. Our neighbour had already shown them over the bungalow. Yes, it was just what they wanted, but the price was a bit high. While this price haggle was going on, the other prospective buyer telephoned, wanting to come over. When the first buyer realised that someone else was interested he offered to pay the full amount on the spot, so the sale was agreed exactly as Christine had said.

Our buyers were anxious to move in so once again we were faced with the problem of finding somewhere to live, but we eventually found a terraced cottage in Loughton. We moved in in January, having left Denton in heavy snow and arrived at Loughton in pouring rain. After the long journey, and because of the limited time of working, the removal men finished up by piling all they had left in the lounge, leaving it to us to sort out after they had gone. Some of our Music Hall friends called in and, seeing the mess, swept us off to a party they had arranged for us. We had a super evening among about fifteen of our friends, and they made us feel really welcome. When we got home we were quite ready to fall into bed hardly noticing the chaos of the lounge.

Early the next morning the door bell rang, and the 'fatigue party' reported for duty and, by midday it looked as though we had lived there for quite a while, everything in its place, and reasonably tidy, except that, as Christine had said, Tara did not move back with us. Her time had come to move on, and we were glad her last memories were of the home she loved, and the freedom she enjoyed there.

Cancer patients were still our great concern, and Ann and I

approached one of the consultants at the Royal London Homoeopathic Hospital with a view to having a group there. He agreed to this, and we started with patients commuting from Dover, Norfolk, Ross-on-Wye and Hertford, in addition to London. This group went along smoothly for nine months until our colleague, Dr Lambert Mount, resigned to go to New Zealand. The man appointed to take his place was not at all sympathetic to our work, and made things as difficult as possible for us. We would sometimes be kept waiting an hour before a suitable room could be found for us to use. Trolleys would be trundling endlessly past the room, or people talking loudly outside, making meditation impossible. None of this had happened before, so it was only too obvious we were not welcome. We did not mind for ourselves, but some of the patients had made long journeys to be with us.

We decided to look for alternative accommodation, and my late secretary, Eileen Hambling, saw an advertisement for rooms for hire in the Nature Cure Clinic off Marylebone Road in London. We went along and saw the secretary, and they made us welcome. The accommodation was excellent, and the doctors working there were most cooperative. When the nursing sister at the Clinic heard about our cancer group, she asked if she might sit in on a session. She did and, very soon, she became part of the group making every effort to create the right atmosphere with flowers, and generally making us all feel at home. After a very short while I was invited to join their consultants, not only for cancer patients, but also for psychotherapy and healing. I did two days a week in that capacity, and the cancer group met every fortnight, with Ruth acting as sister's assistant, looking after the doctors and other practitioners' needs. We had a very pleasant working relationship with the staff and practitioners for two years, during which time I gave a number of lectures on our cancer group work, as well as stress management and spiritual healing. At the Nature Cure Clinic we all had to agree to a vegetarian diet which did not bother us because we liked vegetarian food but, if eating out with friends, we did not embarrass our hosts by refusing to eat meat – we would accept whatever they had prepared for us. I favour a sensible diet but most people whom I have met who have been fanatical about their diet have, sooner or later, had to revert to a more normal one. Once we met a vegan couple, and although Ruth had been ill with a 'flu virus for four weeks, she still looked healthier than the vegans.

In 1979 I had a request for help from a colleague in Scotland whose eleven-year-old daughter was suffering from splintering bones in both knees which was both painful and had put a stop to her ballet which was her great love. He brought her down to see me for a week of treatment which included mental visualisation by 'seeing' the splintered bones knitting and the healthy function of the knees again together with spiritual healing. On her return home she made a practice of 'linking up' with me at nine o'clock each evening for absent healing. After two months, X-rays showed both knees greatly improved and a further two months gave complete freedom of use with healthy bone structure and a return to dancing and horse riding.

Actress Barbara Windsor also had a quick response to healing after twisting her back on location resulting in excrutiating pain for several days. On returning home after treatment she realised she could bend down to take off her boots without pain for the first time in over a week and after one more treatment was happily back at work again.

I was invited to talk to the sixth form at the County Secondary School in Bungay on spiritual healing. It was scheduled for three o'clock until four o'clock in the afternoon. At five-thirty the headmaster came in to say we must close the discussion, or some of the students would miss their bus home. Not only were the questions asked very intelligent, searching ones, but there was so much interest in the subject too. Talking to some of them, it came out that the whole form of some forty students all did valuable community work for the elderly or disabled, shopping, cleaning, gardening, anything that needed doing they would get on with without fuss or bother. Just a good bunch of youngsters one could be proud of.

It has been my contention for a long time that if meditation were to be introduced into school curricula from an early age onwards, we would produce a better quality of youth with a more spiritual, caring nature, like the quiet ones today who contribute something useful to life without making a noise about it. We often look back to those early days of our spiritual unfoldment at the Temple of the Trinity in Palmers Green with Mrs Eva Rayner, and her spirit control Dr Lewis from whom we learned so much. These two lovely souls shaped our lives into the useful pattern that has unfolded over the years, enabling us to pass on that knowledge and experience to several hundred seekers, who have also been directed into a life of service to the sick, suffering and bereaved. Rather like dropping a pebble into a pool – the eddies go on and out to cover the whole surface of the water. So does the philosophy and help of the Holy Spirit extend ever onwards.

After moving back to Loughton, in addition to my work at the Nature Cure Clinic, I also had a clinic at home and, although I had a consulting room, many of my patients with mental, or emotional problems, would need to have someone bring them, which would mean Ruth would have to be with them in the lounge, as there was no space for a waiting room. After two years of this she was getting a bit fed up with the restriction, and we had been looking out for a larger house, without much success. On one of our visits back to Denton, we decided, on the spur of the moment, to extend our visit for a few days, and see if there was anything suitable in that area. We went into an estate agent's that we knew, and he had a nice detached house in Bungay that he thought had been sold, but there was some hold-up somewhere in the chain with the would-be purchaser. So we went along to see the owners. We managed to persuade them to sell to us, and since we already had a cash buyer for our cottage, there were no hold-ups. So we moved in to 19 Beccles Road, Bungay, where we had the waiting room in the back room, and the consulting room in a very nice sun lounge leading out from it.

It is strange, but it does not seem to matter where we go, people will find us if they need help. Soon after our arrival a lady made an appointment to deal with fear. She had been involved in a serious car accident when just approaching crossroads. A car coming in the opposite direction suddenly veered across the road, and hit them broadside. The driver had had a heart attack, and the impact was such that, had they not been in a Rolls Royce, she certainly would have been killed. The effect of this was an absolute terror when in a car, and particularly at crossroads. She would get into such a panic that she would crawl down on the floor. I treated her for the fear, but she had other problems as well. A badly damaged spine, pinched joints in hip, knee and ankle, and continual pain and violent headaches. Within six weeks we had overcome the pain. In three months her fear had reduced sufficiently for her to cope with reaching crossroads without any panic, but still not quite up to driving herself again. This took about another six visits, after which she had regained her old confidence and outgoing personality.

Another delightful titled lady came with excessively high blood pressure and, during the consultation, it came out that her doctor, who was an old family friend, almost frightened her to death every time she saw him about her blood pressure which, needless to say, shot up even more by his attitude. I taught her relaxation, and correct breathing, and the BP remained normal until she went to the doctor again for her regular check up. I told her to change her doctor. She really could not, he was an old family friend, and she did not want to offend him. I said we would have to see what could be done to change things for the better. In my daily intercessions I asked that conditions might be changed to avoid this regular upsurge of her BP when they met. On her next visit she was radiant. 'What do you think, they have had to split up the practice and take on a new partner, and I am on his panel! He is such a nice kind young man, and was so pleased to see the improvement in my blood pressure. I told him I was learning relaxation with you, and he said, "That is just what you needed. Keep on with it. It is better than all the drugs we have to prescribe, and you can only benefit from it." '

We were able to help her again a little later when she lost her husband, and we helped her over the rather difficult period of readjustment. They had lived a very full and active life together, which came to an abrupt end, and she found the many friends they had made over the years in the county a little difficult to deal with at first, and was glad of our moral support.

Back in Bungay it was inevitable that I should become involved with my old boat building friend, who had his works in an old mill there. The boat trade having become quiet, he had turned his attention to something different. A naturally inventive mind, he devised a means of an easy conversion of a private car into a motor caravan, calling it The Carivan. He built the first prototype on a Jaguar, and designed a complete unit in plywood that would, with the boot lid removed from the car, fit into the well of the boot extending forward over the roof on supports giving space for two sleeping berths, with the galley in the boot area where there was full standing headroom, with steps up to the bunks. With his usual ingenuity of getting the maximum into a minimum of space he had a well-equipped galley, even to washing facilities. I was very impressed with this outfit, and bought an old Ford Cortina, and built a similar unit on it. The beauty of it was that the whole unit could be lifted on, or off, within five minutes, so that either the car, or Carivan, could be available at very short notice. We took these to various county shows, and they aroused considerable interest, but no sales, much to my surprise. I have noticed since, however, that a number have appeared on the market, an exact replica, except they are in fibreglass instead of plywood. In spite of the lack of sales, we had lots of fun running round, showing and demonstrating them. I think the main trouble seemed to be, in spite of several windows fitted in the sleeping section, a lot of people felt claustrophobic with only about two and a half feet headroom over the roof of the car. Apart from these snags, I still feel it is an ideal way for young couples to enjoy touring, with more comfort than a tent can provide.

Talking to one of Ruth's brother's wives one day, she asked if we had ever experienced anything like she had when Stanley, Ruth's youngest brother, died. She was in the kitchen and, looking out over the garden, suddenly it was like a rush of wind, flowers and shrubs were almost flattened for a few seconds, then it returned to normal. Shortly after this she was told that Stanley had died. Asking several neighbours if they had experienced this freak wind, no one else had any knowledge of such an incident. We are sure it was the spirit of her brother, or a message of his transition to the next life; the timing was just right.

We became friendly with the late Derek Neville, the poet and naturalist, when he had the lovely old Attingham Mill in Norfolk. He was a fascinating speaker on nature and bird life, with an uncanny ability of healing animals, and birds in particular. On one of our visits to him he had acquired another swan which he had saved by extracting a piece of metal from its neck and, as a result, it followed him about like a pet dog. He came to our summer school at Corton, and held two hundred people spellbound with his beautiful voice, and talk of his experiences with animals, birds and nature. He was a very delightful person, with a spiritual outlook that attracted me to him immediately.

We started a developing group at Denton and this was the outcome of Ruth's first visit to the hairdresser in Bungay. She took with her a copy of a study course on spiritual healing to read while under the dryer. Seeing the cover, the young hairdresser said, 'Excuse me, but are you interested in that sort of thing?' Then he told her a rather sad, but regretfully, often told story. He had joined a developing circle run by an elderly lady, who had taught him to open himself to spirit, without giving any thought to 'closing down' afterwards. The result was that he was 'a natural' and, as soon as he sat down, often in the salon, a spirit entity would take him over, and he was very worried about what might happen. Ruth told him to come and have a talk with me, and he also brought along a girl who was in the same developing circle because she was too frightened that it might happen to her. So they came along, and we explained the importance of opening, and closing, themselves, and to have set times, and days, when they made contact with their spirit helpers. They must appreciate that, although we look to spirit for help and guidance, they look to us to tell them what is right and wrong by earthly standards. This is a serious association between the two worlds, and not a game to be taken lightly. I spoke to his control explaining the situation, and he thanked us for helping both he, and his instrument, asking if they could be accepted for further teaching.

And so, our developing group started, as had all the others, at the request of those who wished to learn of spiritual truths, and develop whatever spiritual attribute they might have latent within them. Very soon, added to these two, we had Dr Ian Pearce and his wife Ruth, Eric Claxton, a friend of theirs from Diss and his wife, and a farmer's wife from the village. All, I am happy to say, have developed the healing ability, and are doing good work.

Another lady who seems to have followed me about, is Eva Goetz, whom I first met when she had an advanced ovarian cyst. This was cleared without the need for surgery, and she has kept in touch with me ever since – just as has one of our very first cancer group participants for sixteen years, and who every Christmas sends a nice letter and progress report, which I might add, is very gratefully received. Meeting up with some of these early group participants, after a lapse of several years, I have made a point of asking whether they continue with their meditation. The same answer always comes back: 'Oh, yes indeed, it has changed my whole life and outlook. I would never have dreamt such a simple – yet difficult thing to cultivate – could have such a dramatic outcome to one's whole life.'

Although Bungay is quite a pleasant market town on the Norfolk/Suffolk border, as I had a clinic in Bury St Edmunds some thirty miles away, and little local, private work, it seemed that the obvious thing to do was move nearer to my work. The nearest rail link was fifteen miles away, either in Norwich or Diss, and there was a very limited bus service, making it difficult for anyone without their own transport, getting to us. We had a friend living in Thurston, just outside Bury St Edmunds, and she found us a very nice bungalow there, which we bought. This was very convenient for my clinic, and also had a consulting room for patients who wanted to see me there.

Among the people I helped in Thurston was a man who had severe headaches. It turned out he was a cranial osteopath, and very much in sympathy with my ideas. I was able to ease the headaches, but advised him to seek medical advice because they were too frequent, and severe, not to be investigated more fully. Two days later he had a heavy haemorrhaging from the nose, and he was rushed off to casualty. X-rays showed a large tumour between the eyes, and radiotherapy was the only answer. His wife rang me asking what they should do. The consultant had not been very reassuring – the treatment might affect the sight, and would cause burning of the tongue and throat. I said to go ahead with the treatment, but tell him to keep it in his mind while having radiation that it was only going to disperse the tumour, and *would not* have any adverse effects on either sight, tongue or throat. I would come over and see him at intervals while the treatment was being given.

He had two sessions of radiation without any apparent problems, then I went over to see him at Ipswich, giving him further healing, saying I would call again in two days. On the next visit, while I was healing him, he gave a start. I asked what was the matter and he said that something like an explosion had happened in his head. Shortly after this he was able to breathe through his nose for the first time in weeks, and it was obvious the tumour was breaking up. I suggested he saw the consultant radiologist when he went for his next treatment, to see if they would X-ray again, and see what had happened. They did so, and found the tumour had gone. Both he, and the consultant, were very pleased with this result and, as there was only one more radiotherapy session to complete the course, he went in for this last session so elated with the result that he forgot to put up his mental defence against possible adverse effects, with the result that his tongue and throat were badly burned, and it was several months before he cleared this effect. Now, who, or what prompted me to suggest he should put up this mental defence? I thought it was pure guess work on my part but, at the same time, I was beginning to learn a little of the power of the mind in relation to our bodily control.

Many of the great medical discoveries have been found accidentally when looking for something quite different. Or is it accidental? I am fairly sure that these are inspired thoughts put into our minds at the right time, and this particular one has been of great value, not only with radiotherapy, but it has also been applied to cases of chemotherapy where the patients have gone through the whole course without the usual nausea and loss of hair normally associated with this treatment. Thus we are just beginning to understand a little of the amazing potential of thought and mind power.

The individual reaction of each person has really been an education for us and I have learned so much from them. A veterinary friend called in one day to ask if we would try and help the Golden Retriever of a friend of hers. It was having fits which had got progressively worse, and were occurring several times a day. They could do nothing for her, and wondered if we could help. Ruth got down on the floor and started whispering sweet nothings in the dog's ear. She quietened down, and we were able to get on with the healing without further troubles. This became a ritual every time she came for healing because she had to have her 'doggie fairy stories'. This went on for quite a long time, and she was managing to go for two to three weeks without a fit. Then the time came when we had to move on once more, and the owner asked if Ruth would make her a tape that they could play to the dog if she got restless. So Ruth made this tape of 'doggie fairy stories', and they took it home. They left it in a room with the dog, switched it on, and left the room, just leaving the door ajar so they could watch what happened. As soon as the voice started she went over to the recorder, put her head down and listened, sat down head on one side as though she was taking it all in, and she did not move until it had finished, when she rolled on her back, and went to sleep. They said they almost cried to see how she reacted, as though she understood every word, and the implication behind it.

We had been at Thurston for about eighteen months when I got a call to speak at a seminar in Bexhill on our cancer work. This proved to be a very pleasant day and, at the end of the afternoon, having met a number of old friends from our NFSH days, several made the comment that we should be there in Bexhill: 'You are just the chap we need with your experience.'

About a month after our return home I had a letter from a woman in Bexhill. She began: 'You won't know me, but I was on the bookstall at the Manor Barn Seminar, and I heard someone saying something about you possibly coming to live in Bexhill. I hope you will forgive me, but I have just heard of a very large flat becoming available, which I think would be ideal for what you want. It is to rent and, if you are interested, the agents are . . .', and she gave me the name and telephone number. We had our friend, Pat Venn, from Australia staying with us at the time, and she thought it sounded interesting and suggested that we take a look. It was a lovely old, detached house, on a corner site, owned by two elderly sisters. It had previously been an hotel and, getting too much for them to manage, had been converted into flats. They each had a flat on the ground floor. The first floor covered the whole area of the house, comprising a very large lounge, dining room, three bedrooms, kitchen, bathroom and two toilets, and this was available to us at a very reasonable rent. The top floor was occupied by a couple near enough our own age. It certainly was a very nice flat and, putting it to the vote, we decided to take it.

Talking it over on the way home, we decided that if we sold the bungalow in Thurston and invested the money, we would be able to buy again later when the need arose. (Little did we know how ridiculously property prices would rocket during the next few years, so that renting proved to be the biggest mistake of our lives, making it impossible to get back into the buying market again.) However, we moved in, and I got together with Leslie Baker who was chairman of the very strong Sussex Healing Association, with the idea of trying to find suitable premises to open a natural health centre and cancer counselling group. Nothing seemed to present itself that was suitable, then one of the sisters (who owned our flat) died. When the upset of the funeral had settled, the surviving sister asked if we knew anyone who might want her sister's flat, and I suggested we might rent it, and use it as a clinic. She hedged a bit for a while probably thinking, 'It's better the devil you know than the one you don't', then she agreed. We then had to get planning permission from the council for its change of use, which was finally granted, with the proviso that it had to be completely insulated against fire. This alone cost another £3,000 but, at last, it was functional, with two treatment rooms, reception and waiting room, toilets and hydrotherapy unit.

Bexhill, having the highest proportion of its population aged over eighty in the United Kingdom, I anticipated no shortage of patients, but strangely, this did not prove to be the case. It seemed they had all got so into the habit of getting their pills from the doctor on a regular basis, they had no inclination to change this procedure, although we had a homoeopath, medical herbalist, psychotherapist, reflexologist, hydrotherapist, counsellor and healers in attendance regularly.

The cancer clinic met as a group bi-weekly, and with Leslie and Gladys Baker assisting both in the Bexhill group, and in one we opened in Hove. Both of these went quite well with an average of four to five patients and their partners, where possible. I was invited to talk to the nurses at the Royal East Sussex Hospital on our cancer work, and I was received with considerable enthusiasm, with the Sister Tutor asking if I would have a group in the hospital. I agreed to do this, and she asked the consultant if they could have it, but this request was met with a flat refusal, saying that he did not want 'that nonsense' in the hospital. This was so typical of the reaction of many medical men, particularly in the higher echelons of consultancy. Anything slightly 'off beat' to their thinking is a non-starter irrespective of any possible value it might have if given some consideration and thought.

Then, after a year or so, first one practitioner, then another, started to drop away from the centre with so little work to do, until I was left almost on my own to try and meet the cost of running the centre which others had put money into to try and keep it solvent. One of my regrets was that some of our friends had put money into this project, particularly Leslie Baker, and it looked as if it was slowly, but surely, getting the better of us.

Soon after we opened the centre a medium friend, Andreas Vasilou offered to put on a meeting at the White Rock Pavilion in Hastings, to both publicise and raise funds for the centre. I would give the talk on our work, and he and Jessie Nason clairvoyance. The meeting was well attended, and quite a lot of interest was shown in what we were offering the locality. A day or two after the meeting I received a letter from a woman who had attended the meeting. She was a nurse, and was extremely interested in our centre, and offered help if we could make use of her training. We met and, although she (Nicky) and her husband (Reg), also a trained nurse, ran a rest home in Bexhill, and lived a pretty full life, she gave us much of her time and expertise, which was invaluable, particularly with the cancer patients, and they have both become very dear friends over the years.

Their rest home was comparatively small, and could not support full-time staff, so that they could never get out together, and they were looking for larger property. Nothing was available in the Hastings district, and they had been looking further afield when, through a relative, they found an ideal house in Newbury, Berkshire, where they had once lived. They bought it and, reluctantly, we said goodbye but, at the same time, feeling it was not goodbye. There was a lot of work to be done on Woodridge, their new home, and we spent a few weekends there – Ruth fitting curtains, while I helped Reg, laying carpets and the hundred-and-one odd jobs that had to be done, but we enjoyed it.

When they had been there about a year, and were nicely established with some twenty residents, I had a call from Nicky. The minister was there and had been telling them the sad story of one of his young parishioners who was dying from cancer. Nicky had mentioned what we did and he asked if we could do anything for Louise. I agreed to help, if the parents wished it. Shortly after this I had a call from Louise's father. He did not think she was well enough to make the journey to Bexhill but, if we could help in any way, they would be very grateful. We went to Newbury next weekend, and met a very delightful young lady. Louise was really making the best use of what life she had and, as yet, had not been told she had passed the time of her diagnosed death. She knew she had cancer but that was not going to interfere with her life, if she could help it. Having explained our therapy she was anxious to get started on it, and we had three daily sessions over the weekend, before returning home. Nicky, our nurse friend who had worked closely with me at Bexhill, and being fully conversant with the therapy, was more than willing to carry on in between my visits. Although Louise was physically weak, her will and determination were very strong. It had been obvious when we first met, she was nearing the end of her earthly journey, but we were able to help her over those last few months, and I like to think we helped her family to accept her passing, not as the end of her life, but rather the promotion to a better and fuller one, freed of the confines of a sick physical body. That she would still be near them with her love. When she was near the end her mother decided it was time to tell her that two years ago they had been told by the specialist she could not live for more than six months. To which Louise replied: 'Do you mean to tell me I've passed my 'O' levels, been away to boarding school and passed my driving test, and I should have been dead? Whoopee, isn't that marvellous!' I wonder how many of us could face this sort of situation in such a stoic manner?

Shortly before she passed away she said to Nicky: 'I had longed to stand on a platform with Gilbert, and tell people how much they can help themselves over illness, but I will still be with him in his work.' Louise loved rainbows and butterflies and on the day of the funeral, quite out of season, a butterfly flew out of the church porch in front of her mother. Do you think that had any significance? An advanced spiritual being occupying a young physical body, here to teach us how life should be lived, with love, compassion and true understanding, I suggest. We have learned so much from Louise, and children like her, that has enhanced our lives. In her seventeen years she was loved by everyone. What a wonderful experience, and what a privilege, to be chosen to bring such a child into the world.

Shortly after the funeral, Louise's parents, Peter and Barbara Callow, wrote saying they would like to become more involved in our work and asked what they could do. I suggested we might hold a meeting in Newbury, and see what the reaction of the town would be to the possible opening of a cancer help centre there and, if so, it would be nice to have it in Louise's memory. The meeting was arranged in one of the school halls when two of my medical colleagues, Dr Lambert Mount from the London Homoeopathic Hospital and Dr Ann Woolley-Hart, medical scientist from St Bartholomew's Hospital, and myself, would talk on cancer help. We had a most successful meeting, with some two hundred people attending. Among the audience was a local doctor who welcomed the idea. Also we had printed some slips on which people could indicate whether they would be interested in giving their support, either with finance, work in any form, fund raising, or any other form of help that might be useful. At the conclusion of the meeting we collected over seventy offers of help from nurses, counsellors, healers and people willing to wash up, clean or do odd jobs of which there are always plenty. So the Louise Callow Cancer Help Centre was going to get off the ground. A committee was formed, and fund raising was obviously high on the agenda, and we soon had a very active team together on this behalf.

The next offer of help came from Louise's headmistress. She ran a nice school, standing in its own grounds on the outskirts of the town. She said that we could have the use of the school any time outside school hours for meetings, use the grounds for fund raising events, and the children themselves would also do some fund raising for us. Among those offering help was a retired nurse and social worker, Peggy Gallagher, who was interested in the group therapy work, and came along with me on this when the group got together. Two important aspects of the centre were now established – a good fund raising team, and the group therapy which helped the participants to come to terms with their illness, and help to cope with it in a constructive way.

Peter Callow was a tower of strength getting things together, and seemed to know everyone worth knowing in the town and surrounding area. We had been trying to get premises for a headquarters. And with all this activity in Newbury it was obvious we needed to be nearer than one hundred and twenty miles away and Reg, our friend at Woodridge, rang saying there was a mobile home for sale at Thatcham. I rang the owner, and we went along to see it. It was a large double unit, square like a bungalow, with a nice garden, and on a corner site. It had a large lounge, kitchen with dining suite, three bedrooms and bathroom/toilet. We could just afford to buy it, so we did. It is strange but, whenever a move is pending, my work tapers off, so that with Leslie and Gladys Baker carrying on with the cancer groups, I was glad of an offer by a young man to take over the clinic in Bexhill. He took over the lease, and signed an agreement for the premises, and all seemed fine. However, nine months later he took off to America, having sold all our furniture, and owing me £750, since when no one has seen or heard of him.

Peter rang me one morning to ask if I could meet him to look at some premises we had been offered. It was on a new industrial estate between Newbury town and Thatcham, over an engineering works, comprising the whole of the upper floor – a very large area – and was occupied by the boss, his desk and a telephone. He had read of our plea for premises and thought how silly it was for him to have so much space while we needed it more than he did. We could have it free, divide it up if we wanted, and all we needed to supply was our own telephone and furniture. So we partitioned off one end into three consulting rooms, leaving a main area large enough to seat fifty people, with a kitchen and toilet at the other end. This enabled us to hold our meetings, counselling consultations and groups, all under the one roof.

At the same time that we had our initial meeting, one of the doctors who attended was working on similar lines for Cancer Care with the launching of the Newbury and District Cancer Care Trust and the Macmillan Nursing Team. Both groups have worked hard, providing special equipment, funds and training to enable patients to be cared for at home, rather than have to go into hospital. The Louise Callow Centre also opened a shop in the town as an information centre for help and advice on all avenues of help available to cancer patients, and their families, with books and literature covering these aspects. In addition a holiday home was provided where patient and family could have a holiday and rest.

The two organisations have worked so closely together for the benefit of the local community that they have recently merged together as the Rainbow Trust to raise funds for the local hospital which has resulted in a fourth room being converted for use by seriously ill patients, and their partners or families. A very rewarding six years' work for all those involved with these projects, and a fitting tribute to a young lady I was privileged to know.

We wanted to register the Louise Callow Cancer Help Centre as a charity and, having been involved with this on two previous occasions, knew only too well how drawn out this process can be, so we decided to complete the application, and to present it in person. We presented it at the Charity Commission and our original application was uncovered from the bottom of a huge pile and, with a bit of flannel on our part, the Commission promised to speed it on its way to the Central Registry, but could not say how long it would sit there before being attended to. A couple of weeks went by, and we had previously written to Prince Charles asking for his support, knowing of his interest in alternative medicine and non-toxic therapies. He replied, saying he was too heavily committed to take on any more charities, but was sending us a donation, asking us not to disclose the amount. This would be sent on receipt of our charity registration number. So I rang the Charity Commission to say that Prince Charles was waiting for our registration number so that he could give us a donation, and this resulted in our receiving the registration number – and Prince Charles's cheque.

14

LOOKING AFTER OURSELVES AT LAST

For the past twenty-five years I have been teaching in various parts of Germany, Austria and Switzerland, and it is gratifying to find so much interest in healing and the many other forms of complementary, and alternative, therapy that we are able to bring to them. We, in England, have so much more freedom of expression than they, particularly where spiritual healing is concerned. Ours is the only country where it can be practised openly with the full approval of the government, and healers are accepted in the majority of our National Health hospitals to counsel and heal the sick.

Now, with over forty years' healing experience behind me, and eight moves in the last sixteen years, lecturing and setting up cancer help centres, and support groups in this country, Gemany, Austria and Switzerland, I felt that now that I am in my eighties Ruth and I might take life a little easier, and be allowed to settle in one place for the remainder of our material lives. We had returned to Bexhill in Sussex for the third time, rather foolishly we now realise, as the high winds prevalent there had an adverse effect on Ruth's health, causing breathing difficulties in particular, so it was obvious this was not to be our settlement area, and that we needed to find a more suitable location. These thoughts set the wheels in motion by our friends 'upstairs' and, over a period of two months we had no less than five different mediums tell us we would be moving away from Bexhill, the last one coming from a medium on one of my infrequent visits to the spiritualist church. She singled me out for the first message saying, 'I see you are surrounded by books – they are telling me you are writing a book. . . .get it to the publishers, it is important this is done, you have much useful knowledge to impart to others.' Various other things with the message were so accurate we decided we would have a private sitting with her – she was Teresa Doherty of St Leonards-on-Sea, and the evidence she gave was really outstanding.

She spoke first about my writing, saying that it should concentrate on three aspects – my life story, the technical side of healing and inspirational writing. Also, my future work would be in three areas – writing, opening a training centre and public speaking. She also mentioned a fourth area – something close to my heart which is my teaching on the continent – but in future the trainees should come to me. She told me I must make out my training programmes because I would be in my new centre by the end of the year, and that I would know when I had found the right place when I found a watermill. Ruth and I had talked about this final move, and decided we would like to get back to Newbury where we had many friends, and her health had been better when we had lived there before.

Teresa Doherty also told us that we would be going to Cavendish Square shortly. I did not know anyone in Cavendish Square so took that with a pinch of salt until two weeks later I had an invitation to a meeting in Cavendish Square. The first time this organisation had ever used this venue.

Teresa then said that she had a very powerful gentleman with her who turned out to be Harry Edwards. She also brought our very dear friend Nan Mackenzie, and Albert Denton who had been the administrator designate for the NFSH, but passed away just before he was due to take up this office. She also brought through Douglas Bader, the legless RAF fighter pilot, and Edward Bach who expressed an interest in our work, telling me to look out for a special flower which would help in our work. Many other people were brought through, some had been patients, some friends, or relatives, but all with strong evidence of their own personalities.

We were also reminded of a donkey sanctuary that we supported, and where we had helped heal the donkeys years ago, and Silver, the 'wonder horse' that our Norfolk friends rescued, and we were able to heal. My father came through, and was very military of stature, which was him to a 'T'. He had never got out of the military walk and bearing from the First World War.

We were told that we were going to be invited to something of a spiritual nature, and the centre would have some religious background. We would have two sets of legal papers to sign, they would be identical, and in 1991 we would be going to Canada and America in conjunction with the work, and also the book promotion. These are the main points from an hour of uninterrupted talking on her part, and this is what has materialised from it, to date, in two months.

Having decided we would try and get back to Newbury to live, if possible, we arranged to spend a few days there visiting our friends, and looking at possible properties, remembering that we had dropped out of the buying market many years ago. We wrote off for a list of hotels and guest houses in the area. When this arrived I was rather taken aback by the prices. In Bexhill we had numerous good guest houses with charges for bed and breakfast ranging from £12 to £20 per night. In Newbury they started at £56 going up to £100. Going through the list, one caught my eye – 'An Art and Healing Centre'. This not only looked promising by the description, but the prices were more reasonable too. I telephoned, and booked ourselves in for a week. We arrived at 'Westridge' a lovely old manor house, standing in its own grounds. We went in and, on a beautiful old oak carved table in the hall, was some literature, and the first to catch my eye were leaflets advertising the Newbury theatre which is called the Watermill Theatre. We had been told to look for a watermill and, when we found it, that is where we should be. Talking to the owner, we discovered that her mother, who had died five years ago, had been a well-known healer in the area, and the owner wanted to carry on her work. In conversation during our stay, I mentioned that I was looking for accommodation to open a teaching centre, and she said, 'Well now, my mother started negotiations to buy a chapel next door but one, and the Trust took so long to finalise it, I have only just completed the purchase and, of course, I can let it to whomsoever I like.'

Again, we were told our centre would have a religious background, and here was an old Congregational Chapel waiting for us. All this seemed to be fitting into place so easily but, now came the biggest problem. We would need somewhere permanent to live. We visited every estate agent in the town with very little hope of finding rented accommodation. We got the names of all housing associations in the area – only two would even put our name on a long waiting list, one of which was the Council Housing Association who had previously turned us down. We returned home feeling we had, at least, succeeded with half of the project, and, if the worst came to the worst, we could live at Westridge until we found a flat.

Three weeks later I had to go to Shrewsbury to check on three groups of healers who had applied for full membership of the World Federation of Healing. Two days before we went there I met a medium friend in the town, and he said that he was coming up to Shrewbury with me because he had been booked in to give some sittings there.

While there, I spent my time between Shrewsbury, Newtown and Welshpool, and he remained in Shrewsbury. He stayed on a day longer than Ruth and me and, on the evening before we left he said that he had started an aurograph for us and that there was some news on the way for us and that, when we got home there would be some pleasant surprises.

We had a rotten journey home, arriving two and a half hours late and, feeling a little frayed around the edges, we pushed our way through a pile of letters and other rubbish on the floor, put the kettle on for a cup of tea, switched on the heater for a shower, only to find it would not light because the ignition switch was broken – pleasant surprises he had said. We had our cup of tea, looked at the pile of mail, and the flashing answerphone, wondering what to do first. I went through the mail and there was a letter from a publisher asking to see the manuscript of the book. Then we tackled the twenty-odd messages on the answerphone, and one was from Newbury to say that one of the housing trusts had a two-bedroom flat available, and if we were interested we were to go for an interview. We could not believe it – we had not expected to find anything before next year, and it was all happening in a matter of weeks. So we went back to Newbury for the interview, saw the flat and liked it, and were told that the Trust would discuss our application and let us know their verdict. I asked the secretary, who took us over the flat a second time before we left, why we should be so lucky as to have this offer when we had only been on the list for two months. She said that it was strange, but it was the first empty flat for several years, and this only happened because the outgoing tenant had agreed an exchange, and the people who were coming changed their minds at the last moment. She then said that she had not realised until she met a mutual friend, that I was the person who was responsible for setting up the cancer centre in Newbury, and she felt they owed it to me to do something in return.

On arrival home next day, there was a message on the answerphone saying the Trust would be pleased to have us as tenants. The two sets of identical documents to sign, as foretold by Teresa Doherty, were the papers for the flat. Then we were told that the training centre that was to be, would be known as the Gilbert Anderson Training Centre, and that I should start making out training courses.

We have now established cancer groups in Graz and Vienna in Austria, Bern and Zurich in Switzerland, and a special group in the Black Forest, comprising doctors, practitioners and healers, where individuals come each year to learn our method, and use it in their own practices in many different parts of Germany, in addition to the thirty or so, resulting from our teaching seminars in this country.

In mid-1991 I completed my four-year term as President of the World Federation of Healing, giving me more time to devote to the building up of this new teaching centre at Westridge, Highclere and Cliff House, Cromer, where others will be able to carry on after I have to resign myself to the inevitable, and move on to a new phase of life.

Looking back now over the first half of my life, I do not think that I achieved anything spectacular – perhaps I was a little better off financially, but I cannot say that this gave us any great satisfaction. But I must say that, with the help and guidance from our many friends in the other world, our lives have certainly been enriched in their second halves, and we feel we have contributed something of use to the community at large.

Sadly, many of our old colleagues and friends have moved on ahead of us, but I look forward with the knowledge we will meet again in due course, and I must say I feel so sorry for those who do not have this same knowledge of the continuity of life and the tremendous help and guidance available to us, if only we have the sense to open our minds to this greater sphere of life when the two worlds intermingle, if we do not close the door on it. It is my intention to endeavour to unite the two worlds more closely together in my next book by sharing our experiences, and the wisdom that has been imparted to us over the past forty-five years' contact with many learned souls in spirit.